Helping Students Understand Algebra

By
BARBARA SANDALL, Ed.D., and MARY SWARTHOUT, Ph.D.

COPYRIGHT © 2005 Mark Twain Media, Inc.

ISBN   10-digit: 1-58037-293-7
       13-digit: 978-1-58037-293-0

Printing No. CD-404020

Mark Twain Media, Inc., Publishers
Distributed by Carson-Dellosa Publishing Company, Inc.

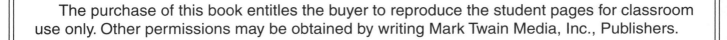

Table of Contents

Table of Contents (cont.)

Introduction

The *Helping Students Understand Algebra Series* will introduce students in middle school through high school to the topics of Pre-Algebra, Algebra I, and Algebra II. All of the worktexts will be aligned with the National Council of Teachers of Mathematics (NCTM) *Principles and Standards for School Mathematics.*

This series is written for classroom teachers, parents, families, and students. The worktexts in this series can be used as a full unit of study or as individual lessons to supplement textbooks or curriculum programs. Parents and students can use this series as an enhancement to what is being done in the classroom or as a tutorial at home. All students will benefit from these activities, but the series was designed for the struggling math student in mind. The **concepts and explanations** for the concepts are described in simple **step-by-step instructions** with **examples** in the introduction of each lesson. Students will be given practice problems using the concepts introduced and descriptions of real-life applications of the concepts.

According to the Mathematics Education Trust and the NCTM, new technologies require that the fundamentals of algebra and algebraic thinking should be a part of the background for all citizens. These technologies also provide opportunities to generate numerical examples, graph data, analyze patterns, and make generalizations. An understanding of algebra is also important because business and industry require higher levels of thinking and problem solving.

NCTM *Standards* suggest content and vocabulary are necessary, but of equal importance are the processes of mathematics. The process skills described in the *Standards* include: problem solving, reasoning, communication, and connections. The worktexts in the series will address both the content and the processes of algebra and algebraic thinking. This worktext, *Helping Students Understand Algebra,* will help students continue their transition from arithmetic to algebra.

Principles and Standards for School Mathematics, NCTM

Number and Operations

Students will be enabled to:

- Understand numbers, ways of representing numbers, relationships among numbers, and number systems.
- Understand meanings of operations and how they relate to one another.
- Compute fluently and make reasonable estimates.

Algebra

Students will be enabled to:

- Understand patterns, relations, and functions.
- Represent and analyze mathematical situations and structures using algebraic symbols.
- Use mathematical models to represent and understand quantitative relationships.
- Analyze change in various contexts.

Geometry

Students will be enabled to:

- Analyze characteristics and properties of two- and three-dimensional geometric shapes and develop mathematical arguments about geometric relationships.
- Specify locations and describe spatial relationships using coordinate geometry and other representational systems.
- Apply transformations and use symmetry to analyze mathematical situations.
- Use visualization, spatial reasoning, and geometric modeling to solve problems.

Measurement

Students will be enabled to:

- Understand measurable attributes of objects and the units, systems, and processes of measurement.
- Apply appropriate techniques, tools, and formulas to determine measurements.

Data Analysis and Probability

Students will be enabled to:

- Formulate questions that can be addressed with data and collect, organize, and display relevant data to answer them.
- Select and use appropriate statistical methods to analyze data.
- Develop and evaluate inferences and predictions that are based on data.
- Understand and apply basic concepts of probability.

NCTM Standards and Expectations
Grades 9–12 Algebra, NCTM

Algebra instructional programs from grades 9 through 12 should enable all students to:

Understand patterns, relations, and functions
- Generalize patterns using explicitly defined and recursively defined functions;
- Understand relations and functions and select, convert flexibly among, and use various representations of them;
- Analyze functions of one variable by investigating rates of change, intercepts, zeroes, asymptotes, and local and global behavior;
- Understand and perform transformations, such as arithmetically combining, composing, and inverting commonly used fractions, and using technology to perform such operations on more complicated symbolic expressions;
- Understand and compare the properties of classes of functions, including exponential, polynomial, rational, logarithmic, and periodic functions; and
- Interpret representations of functions of two variables.

Represent and analyze mathematical situations and structures using algebraic symbols
- Understand the meaning of equivalent forms of expressions, equations, inequalities, and relations;
- Write equivalent forms of equations, inequalities, and systems of equations and solve them with fluency—mentally or with paper and pencil in simple cases and using technology in all cases;
- Use symbolic algebra to represent and explain mathematical relationships;
- Use a variety of symbolic representations, including recursive and parametric equations, for functions and relations; and
- Judge the meaning, utility, and reasonableness of the results of symbol manipulations, including those carried out by technology.

Use mathematical models to represent and understand quantitative relationships
- Identify essential quantitative relationships in a situation and determine the class or classes of functions that might model the relationships; and
- Use symbolic expressions, including interactive and recursive forms, to represent relationships arising from various contexts.

Analyze change in various contexts
- Approximate and interpret rates of change from graphical and numerical data.

Common Mathematics Symbols and Terms

Term	Symbol/Definition	Example
Addition sign	$+$	$2 + 2 = 4$
Subtraction sign	$-$	$4 - 2 = 2$
Multiplication sign	x or a dot • or 2 numbers or letters together or parenthesis	3×2 $2 \bullet 2$ $2x$ $2(2)$
Division sign	$\div$ or a slash mark (/) or a horizontal fraction bar, or $\sqrt{}$	$6 \div 2$ $4/2$ $\frac{4}{2}$ $2\overline{)4}$
Equals or is equal to	$=$	$2 + 2 = 4$
Does Not Equal	$\neq$	$5 \neq 1$
Parentheses – symbol for grouping numbers	$(\ )$	$(2 \times 5) + 3 =$
Pi – a number that is approximately 22/7 or ≈ 3.14	π	$3.1415926...$
Negative number – to the left of zero on a number line	$-$	-3
Positive number – to the right of zero on a number line	$+$	$+4$
Less than	$<$	$2 < 4$
Greater than	$>$	$4 > 2$
Greater than or equal to	$\geq$	$2 + 3 \geq 4$
Less than or equal to	$\leq$	$2 + 1 \leq 4$
Is approximately	$\approx$	$\pi \approx 3.14$
Radical sign	$\sqrt{}$	$\sqrt{9}$ The square root of 9 $\sqrt[3]{27}$ The cube root of 27
The nth power of a	a^n	$3^2 = 9$

Common Mathematics Symbols and Terms (cont.)

Variables	Are letters used for unknown numbers	$x + 8 = 12$ x is the letter representing the unknown number or variable
Mathematical Sentence	Contains two mathematical phrases joined by an equals (=) or an inequalities ($\neq$, $<$, $>$, $\leq$, $\geq$) sign	$2 + 3 = 5$ $9 - 3 > 5$ $3x + 8 = 20$ $4 + 2 \neq 5$
Equation	Mathematical sentence in which two phrases are connected with an equals (=) sign.	$5 + 7 = 12$ $3x = 12$ $1 = 1$
Mathematical Operations	Mathematics has four basic operations: addition, subtraction, multiplication, and division. Symbols are used for each operation.	+ sign indicates addition – sign indicates subtraction ÷ indicates division • or x indicates multiplication
Like Terms	Can be all numbers or variables that are the same letter and same exponent	3, 4, 5 $3c$, $-5c$, $\frac{1}{2}c$ the variable is the same with the same exponent; they are like terms.
Unlike Terms	Can be numbers or variables that are different	$5 + a$ Cannot be added because they are unlike terms $3x + 4y + 1z$ Cannot be added because the variables are different, so they are unlike terms
Coefficient	The number in front of the variable (letter for the unknown number)	$5x$ In this number, 5 is the coefficient
Identity Property of Addition	Any number or variable added to zero is that number or variable.	$0 + 5 = 5$ $-3 + 0 = -3$ $a + 0 = a$
Identity Property of Multiplication	Any number or variable times 1 is equal to that number or variable.	$12 • 1 = 12$ $b • 1 = b$ $3y • 1 = 3y$

Common Mathematics Symbols and Terms (cont.)

Commutative Property of Addition	No matter the order in which you add two numbers, the sum is always the same.	$4 + 7 = 7 + 4$ $a + b = b + a$
Commutative Property of Multiplication	No matter the order in which you multiply two numbers, the answer is always the same.	$20 \times \frac{1}{2} = \frac{1}{2} \times 20$ $5 \cdot 3 = 3 \cdot 5$ $a \cdot b = b \cdot a$
Associative Property of Addition	When you add three numbers together, the sum will be the same no matter how you group the numbers.	$(5 + 6) + 7 = 5 + (6 + 7)$ $(a + b) + c = a + (b + c)$
Associative Property of Multiplication	No matter how you group the numbers when you multiply, the answer will always be the same product.	$(5 \cdot 4) \cdot 8 = 5 \cdot (4 \cdot 8)$ $(a \cdot b) \cdot c = a \cdot (b \cdot c)$
Distributive Property of Multiplication Over Addition	Allows the choice of multiplication followed by addition or addition followed by multiplication.	$3(5 + 2) = 3 \cdot 5 + 3 \cdot 2$ $a(b + c) = a \cdot b + a \cdot c$
Inverse Operation	Operation that undoes another operation	Multiplication and division $5 \cdot x = 5x$ $\dfrac{5x}{5} = x$ Addition and Subtraction $n + 5 - 5 = n$
Reciprocal or Multiplicative Inverse Property	Two reciprocals are multiplied, and the product is 1.	For any non-zero number: $\text{Number} \times \dfrac{1}{\text{Number}} = 1$ $\dfrac{1}{\text{Number}} \times \text{Number} = 1$ $a \cdot \dfrac{1}{a} = 1$ $5 \cdot \dfrac{1}{5} = 1$

Common Mathematics Symbols and Terms (cont.)

Exponents	Shorthand for repeated multiplication	$a^2 = a \cdot a$ $y^4 = y \cdot y \cdot y \cdot y$
Square Numbers	The result of multiplying a number or variable by itself	$4 \cdot 4 = 16$ $a \cdot a = a^2$
Square Roots	A square root indicated by the radical sign $\sqrt{}$ is the number multiplied by itself to get the radicand.	$\sqrt{9}$ What number multiplied by itself = 9? $3 \cdot 3 = 9$ So $\sqrt{9} = 3$
Radicand	Number under the radical	$\sqrt{9}$ 9 is the radicand
Index	Number inside the radical crook tells how many times the number must be multiplied by itself.	$\sqrt[3]{27}$ 3 is the index What number multiplied by itself 3 times equals the radicand (27)?
Numerator	Top number in a fraction	$\frac{3}{5}$ In this fraction, 3 is the numerator.
Denominator	Bottom number in a fraction	$\frac{3}{5}$ In this fraction, 5 is the denominator.
Integers	Natural numbers, their opposites, or negative numbers, and zero	Set of integers: $\{...-3,-2,-1,0,1,2,3...\}$
Additive Inverse Property of Addition	The sum of an integer and its opposite integer will always be zero.	$a + -a = 0$ $5 + -5 = 0$
Set	Specific group of numbers or objects	Set of integers: $\{...-3,-2,-1,0,1,2,3...\}$
Quadratic Formula	If trying to solve an equation of the form $ax^2 + bx + c = 0$, then $\dfrac{-b \pm \sqrt{b^2 - 4ac}}{2a}$	Find the two unique solutions to any quadratic equation.

Common Mathematics Symbols and Terms (cont.)

Absolute Value	The absolute value of a number can be considered as the distance between the number and zero on the number line.
	
	The absolute value of every number will be either positive or zero.
	
	Real numbers come in paired opposites, a and $-a$, that are the same distance from the origin but in opposite directions.
	
		Absolute value of a:
		   $\|a\| = a$ if a is positive
		   $\|a\| = a$ if a is negative.
		   $\|a\| = 0$ if a is 0
		With 0 as the **origin** on the number line on the left, the absolute value of both -3 and +3 is equal to 3, because both numbers are 3 units in distance from the origin.

Expression	Any collection of numbers, variables, or terms with grouping symbols and mathematical operators.	$-3xy$ $2ab + b$ $2z + 4c + 2 - y$ $5[(x + 3)^2 - 4b] + 2h$
Monomial Expression	A number, variable, or the product of a number and one or more variables raised to whole number powers	a $\frac{1}{2}r$ $-3xy$
Binomial Expression	Has 2 unlike terms combined by an addition or subtraction sign. Sum of number, variable, or the product of a number and one or more variables raised to whole number powers with only two terms	$2x - 9$ $2ab + b$ $x + 3$ $x - 7$
Polynomial Expression	Has 1, 2, 3, or more terms combined by an addition or subtraction sign. Sum of number, variable, or the product of a number and one or more variables raised to whole number powers	$4a + 6$ $x^2 + 5 + 5x$ $z + a + b - a$ $2z + 4c + 2 - y$

Common Mathematics Symbols and Terms (cont.)

Function	The relation of one variable to another. The value of one variable depends on the value of the other variable. A relation in which each input number has one output number A rule that pairs a number from one set with a number in a second set Provides a description of a relationship between two variables, an input variable, and an output variable. The output variable depends on the input variable.	*Example 1:* $d = 0.2t + 2$ *Example 2:* | x	y
-1	0
5	6
0	1
7	8 | Each input value in the x column is paired with exactly one output value in the y column.
---	---	---
Ordered Pair	Describes a point on a graph. The first number in the pair tells the location on the x-axis, and the second tells the location of the point on the y-axis.	(3,8) - three to the right of 0 on the x-axis; 8 up on the y-axis. The point is where these two intersect.
Relation	A set of ordered pairs where the first components of the ordered pair are the input values, and the second are the output values.	(5,10)
Domain	Set of all input values to which the rule applies; (independent variables) the first number in an ordered pair	{(5,6), (10,7)} The set {5,10} is the domain for this rule.
Range	Set of all output values to which the rule applies; (dependent variables) the second number in an ordered pair	{(5,6), (10,7)} The set {6,7} is the range for this rule.
Function Notation	$f(x)$ or f of x	If x is the input variable, and you are looking for the functional value of $f(2)$ for the function of $f(x) = x^4 - 2$, substitute 2 for the x in this rule.

Algebra Rules

Integer Subtraction Rule	For all integers a and b, $a - b = a + \text{-}b$	$10 - 5 = 10 + (\text{-}5)$
Equal Addition Rule	If equal quantities are added to each side of the equation, it does not change the root value of the equation.	$2y - 1 = 6$ $2y - 1 + 1 = 6 + 1$
Equal Subtraction Rule	If equal quantities are subtracted from each side of the equation, it does not change the root value of the equation.	$4x + 2 = 10$ $4x + 2 - 2 = 10 - 2$
Equal Multiplication Rule	If equal quantities are multiplied times each side of the equation, it does not change the root value of the equation.	$\dfrac{x}{6} = 3$ $(6)\dfrac{x}{6} = 3(6)$
Equal Division Rule	If equal quantities are divided into each side of the equation, it does not change the root value of the equation.	$4n = 8$ $\dfrac{4n}{4} = \dfrac{8}{4}$

Chapter 1: Review of Number Systems

Introduction to Number Systems

This section is a review of the basic mathematical concepts needed prior to learning algebra. According to the NCTM *Standards*, students need to be able to:

- Understand numbers, ways of representing numbers, relationships among numbers, and number systems. NCTM.

Galileo said, "[The universe] cannot be read until we have learned the language and become familiar with the characters in which it is written." In order to understand algebra, you need to understand the language of algebra. Algebra uses numbers, symbols, and letters. The numbers used in algebra include the types of numbers described in this section. Different symbols, shown in the chart on the previous pages, mean different things. All of the symbols used in mathematics help describe the numbers or the operations to be done. The letters (variables) used in mathematics represent unknown numbers. This chapter examines types of numbers used in algebra. More detail will be provided as you work your way through this worktext.

Concepts

1 Types of Numbers

    A Natural Numbers

    B Whole Numbers

    C Integers

    D Rational Numbers (Fractions)

    E Irrational Numbers

    F Real Numbers

Explanations of Concepts

1 Types of Numbers

The major types of numbers described in this worktext include natural numbers, whole numbers, integers, rational numbers, irrational numbers, and real numbers.

Chapter 1: Review of Number Systems (cont.)

A Natural Numbers

Natural numbers are sometimes called **counting numbers** because they are the numbers you use to count how many items you have. Zero is not included in the set of natural numbers. TIP: One way to remember this is if you did not have any items, you could not count them.

Example:

Counting the oranges below you would count 1, 2, 3, so you have 3 oranges.

1	2	3	
			= 3 oranges

Examples of Other Natural Numbers:

3	162	1,723	5

Examples of Numbers That Are Not Natural Numbers:

0	0.35	-2	$\frac{4}{7}$

B Whole Numbers

Whole numbers include the natural numbers and zero.

Examples of Whole Numbers:

0	28	1,005

Examples of Numbers That Are Not Whole Numbers:

-2	0.45	$\frac{4}{5}$

11

Chapter 1: Review of Number Systems (cont.)

Look at the number line below. The numbers represented by the equally spaced marks to the right of zero are whole numbers. The arrow on the number line indicates that the line goes on forever, or to infinity. Any number that is between the marks would not be a whole number.

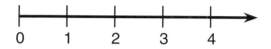

C Integers

Integers are natural numbers, their opposites or negative numbers, and zero. All whole numbers are integers, and all natural numbers can be called integers.

Examples of Integers:

-4   0   -57   2,356   +4

Examples of Numbers That Are Not Integers:

$\frac{1}{2}$ $3\frac{1}{4}$ 0.75   -11.46

Look at the number line below. The negative numbers have been added to the previous number line. The numbers represented by the equally spaced marks to the left or right of zero are integers. Any number represented between the marks is not an integer. For example, 1.5 is not an integer.

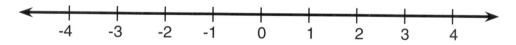

D Rational Numbers (Fractions)

A rational number is a number that can be expressed as the ratio of two integers. This ratio is sometimes called a fraction. The set of rational numbers includes the integers, whole numbers, and natural numbers that were discussed earlier. Decimals are rational numbers if the decimal has a finite number of places in it or it repeats a block of digits infinitely. To find the decimal form of a fraction (in this case $\frac{1}{2}$), divide the numerator (in this case it is 1) by the denominator (in this case it is 2). The decimal form of $\frac{1}{2} = 0.5$.

Chapter 1: Review of Number Systems (cont.)

Examples of Rational Numbers:

3 is a rational number because it can be written as $\frac{3}{1}$.

$\frac{1}{4}$ $-\frac{2}{3}$ 0.35 5.2345 0.5

0.272727… or it can be written as $0.\overline{27}$ as a repeating decimal. It is a rational number because it repeats the same finite block of numbers forever, or to infinity.

Example of a Decimal That Is NOT a Rational Number:

π is the symbol for pi. The decimal form of pi is 3.1415926…

0.01011011101111… and it continues. This pattern never ends, but it does not repeat the same finite block of digits, so it is not a rational number.

E Irrational Numbers

Irrational numbers are numbers that cannot be expressed as a ratio of two integers. The square root of two is an example of an irrational number. An irrational number can be defined as a decimal that never repeats and never ends. The square root of any number that is not a perfect square will be irrational. The square root of 16 ($\sqrt{16}$) is 4, and 4 is a rational number. $\sqrt{3} = 1.7320508$…. This is a decimal that never repeats the same finite block of digits and never ends, so it is an irrational number.

Examples of Irrational Numbers:

$\sqrt{2}$ $\sqrt{3}$

π is the symbol for pi. The decimal form of pi is 3.1415926… .

0.01011011101111… and it continues. This pattern never ends, and it never repeats the same finite block of digits.

1.98342709168032647391084.....

Chapter 1: Review of Number Systems (cont.)

 **Real Numbers**

Real numbers are a combination of all the number systems. Real numbers include natural numbers, whole numbers, integers, rational numbers, and irrational numbers. Examples of real numbers could be any number. Examples of each were shown on the previous pages.

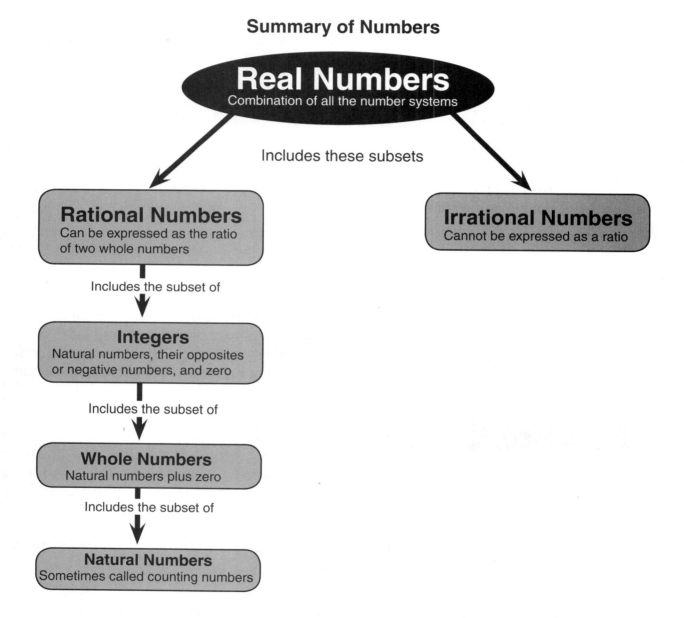

Summary of Numbers

Real Numbers
Combination of all the number systems

Includes these subsets

Rational Numbers
Can be expressed as the ratio of two whole numbers

Irrational Numbers
Cannot be expressed as a ratio

Includes the subset of

Integers
Natural numbers, their opposites or negative numbers, and zero

Includes the subset of

Whole Numbers
Natural numbers plus zero

Includes the subset of

Natural Numbers
Sometimes called counting numbers

Chapter 1: Review of Number Systems (cont.)

Summary of Number Systems

All types of numbers are needed in working to solve problems. Algebra uses numbers, symbols, and letters to solve problems. Types of numbers described in this section include real, rational, irrational, integers, whole, and natural.

- Real numbers are a combination of all the number systems.
- Rational numbers can be expressed as the ratio of two whole numbers.
- Irrational numbers cannot be expressed as a ratio.
- Integers include natural numbers, their opposites or negative numbers, and zero.
- Whole numbers are the natural numbers plus zero.
- Natural numbers are sometimes called counting numbers.

Tip to Remember

An easy way to understand how these number systems fit together is to look at a number line. Real numbers, or all of the number systems discussed in this section, make up all of the numbers represented by the marks with numbers and all of the points in between the marks. Remember that the arrows indicate that this number line goes on into infinity or forever in both directions.

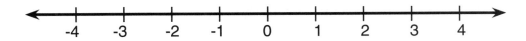

Real Life Applications of Numbers

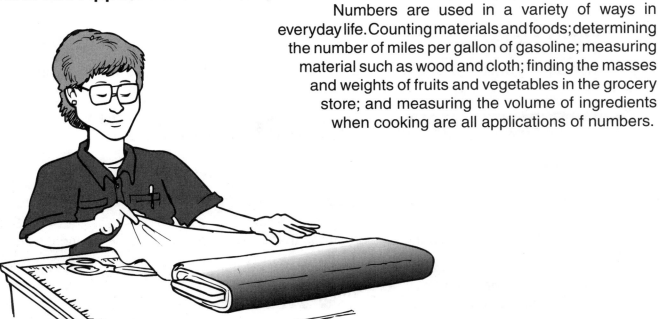

Numbers are used in a variety of ways in everyday life. Counting materials and foods; determining the number of miles per gallon of gasoline; measuring material such as wood and cloth; finding the masses and weights of fruits and vegetables in the grocery store; and measuring the volume of ingredients when cooking are all applications of numbers.

Chapter 2: Review of Properties of Numbers

Introduction to Properties of Numbers

Number operations have certain properties or rules. The properties related to algebra include the Identity Properties, Commutative Properties, and Associative Properties of Addition and Multiplication and the Distributive Property of Multiplication Over Addition.

Concepts of Properties of Numbers

1. Identity Property of Addition
2. Identity Property of Multiplication
3. Commutative Property of Addition
4. Commutative Property of Multiplication
5. Associative Property of Addition
6. Associative Property of Multiplication
7. Inverse Operations
8. Reciprocal or Multiplicative Inverse Property
9. Distributive Property

Identity Properties
Commutative Properties
Associative Properties

Explanations of Concepts of Properties of Numbers

1 Identity Property of Addition

When adding or subtracting zero and any number or variable, the answer is the number or variable.

Examples of Adding or Subtracting Zero From Numbers or Variables:

$$a + 0 = a \qquad 2b - 0 = 2b$$

2 Identity Property of Multiplication

The Identity Property of Multiplication states that any number or variable multiplied by 1 is that number or variable.

Examples of the Identity Property of Multiplication:

$$c \times 1 = c \qquad 1 \times c = c \qquad \text{-}8 \times 1 = \text{-}8$$

Chapter 2: Review of Properties of Numbers (cont.)

3 **Commutative Property of Addition**

The Commutative Property of Addition states that no matter the order in which you add two numbers or algebraic expressions, the sum is always the same.

Examples of the Commutative Property of Addition:

$5 + 6 = 6 + 5$

$5 + 6 = 11$ and $6 + 5 = 11$

Therefore, $5 + 6 = 6 + 5$ because $11 = 11$

$a + b = b + a$

4 **Commutative Property of Multiplication**

The Commutative Property of Multiplication states that no matter the order in which you multiply two numbers or algebraic expressions, the answer is always the same.

Examples of the Commutative Property of Multiplication:

$20 \times \frac{1}{2} = \frac{1}{2} \times 20$

$20 \times \frac{1}{2} = 10$ and $\frac{1}{2} \times 20 = 10$

$10 = 10$

Therefore, $20 \times \frac{1}{2} = \frac{1}{2} \times 20$

$a \cdot b = b \cdot a$

5 **Associative Property of Addition**

The Associative Property of Addition states that when you add three numbers or algebraic expressions together, the sum will be the same no matter how you group them.

Chapter 2: Review of Properties of Numbers (cont.)

Examples of the Associative Property of Addition:

$7 + (9 + 10) = (7 + 9) + 10$

Step 1: Remember, you add the numbers in parentheses first.

$(9 + 10) = 19$ $7 + 9 = 16$

Step 2: Then add the sum and the remaining number on both sides.

$7 + 19 = 26$ $16 + 10 = 26$

$26 = 26$

Therefore, $7 + (9 + 10) = (7 + 9) + 10$.

$a + (b + c) = (a + b) + c$

6 Associative Property of Multiplication

The Associative Property of Multiplication states that when you multiply three numbers or algebraic expressions together, the answer will always be the same no matter how you group them.

Examples of the Associative Property of Multiplication:

$(10 \times 4) \times 5 = 10 \times (4 \times 5)$

Step 1: Remember, you multiply numbers in parentheses first.

$10 \times 4 = 40$ $4 \times 5 = 20$

Step 2: Then multiply what was in the parentheses and the remaining number on both sides.

$40 \times 5 = 200$ $10 \times 20 = 200$

$200 = 200$

Therefore, $(10 \times 4) \times 5 = 10 \times (4 \times 5)$.

$(a \times b) \times c = a \times (b \times c)$

Step 1: Remember, you multiply numbers in parentheses first.

$a \times b = ab$ $b \times c = bc$

Step 2: Then multiply what was in the parentheses and the remaining number on both sides.

$ab \times c = abc$ $a \times bc = abc$

$abc = abc$

Therefore, $(a \times b) \times c = a \times (b \times c)$.

Chapter 2: Review of Properties of Numbers (cont.)

7 **Inverse Operations**

Inverse operations are operations that cancel each other. Addition and subtraction are inverse operations, and multiplication and division are inverse operations.

Examples of Inverse Operations:

$5n - 9$

If you add 9, it undoes subtracting the 9, and you end up with $5n$ again.

$9 - 9 = 0$

The addition undoes the subtraction.

$7 \times n = 7n$

If you divide $7n$ by 7, you undo the multiplication.

$$\frac{7n}{7} = \frac{7}{7} = 1 \text{ so } 1 \times n = n$$

The division undoes the multiplication.

8 **Reciprocal or Multiplicative Inverse Property**

Reciprocal or Multiplicative Inverse Property—any real number has a reciprocal number. When the number and its reciprocal are multiplied together, the product is one.

For any non-zero number

$$\text{Number} \times \frac{1}{\text{Number}} = 1$$

$$\frac{1}{\text{Number}} \times \text{Number} = 1$$

Examples of Reciprocal or Multiplicative Inverse Operations:

$\frac{3}{4}$ is reciprocal of $1\frac{1}{3}$

$1\frac{1}{3} = \frac{4}{3}$

$\frac{3}{4}$ is reciprocal of $\frac{4}{3}$

$$\frac{3}{4} \times \frac{4}{3} = \frac{3 \times 4}{4 \times 3} = \frac{12}{12} = 1$$

Therefore, $\frac{3}{4}$ is the reciprocal of $1\frac{1}{3}$.

Chapter 2: Review of Properties of Numbers (cont.)

1 is its own reciprocal.
$1 \times 1 = 1$
1 is its own reciprocal.

-1 is its own reciprocal.
$-1 \times -1 = 1$
When you multiply two negative numbers, you end up with a positive number as the product.
Therefore, -1 is its own reciprocal.

0 has no reciprocal.
0 times any number is 0.

9 **Distributive Property of Multiplication Over Addition**

This property is usually called the Distributive Property. The basic rule uncovered here is that when you have both the operation of addition and the operation of multiplication to do, you can decide which you want to do first. Suppose you have $3(2 + 5)$ to simplify. Notice that you have addition in the parentheses, and then you need to multiply by 3. So by order of operations, $3(2 + 5) = 3(7) = 21$. But we could do the multiplication first, as long as we distribute. What does this mean? Think about an arrow that links 3 to each part of the addition problem.

$$3(2 + 5) = 3 \times 2 + 3 \times 5 = 6 + 15 = 21$$

Notice that this answer, when we distribute, multiply first, and then add, is the same as our first answer. In general, $a(b + c) = a \times b + a \times c$ for any real numbers.

Examples Using the Distributive Property:

$$3(x + 7) = 3 \bullet x + 3 \bullet 7 = 3x + 21$$

$$b(b + 1) = b \bullet b + b \bullet 1 = b^2 + b$$

Remember the dot • can be used as a multiplication sign.

Distributive Property

Name: _____   Date: _____

Chapter 2: Review of Properties of Numbers (cont.)

Practice: Properties of Numbers

Directions: Solve the problems below and identify which property or properties the problem represents.

Identity Property of Addition   **Identity Property of Multiplication**
Commutative Property of Addition   **Commutative Property of Multiplication**
Associative Property of Addition   **Associative Property of Multiplication**
Reciprocal or Multiplicative Inverse Property   **Inverse Operations**
Distributive Property

	Simplify	**Operation**
1. $x + 0 =$	x	identity
2. $b \cdot 1 =$	b	identity
3. $\frac{1}{5} \times 0 = 0 \times \frac{1}{5}$	0	commutative
4. $3y \cdot 7 = 7 \cdot 3y$	$21y$	commutative
5. $a + b = b + a$	how?	commutative
6. $(3 + 9) + 7 = 3 + (9 + 7)$	19	associative
7. $5 \cdot x$ and $\frac{5x}{5} =$	$5x$	recripocal
8. $(d \cdot b) \cdot c = d \cdot (b \cdot c)$	dbc	distributive
9. $x - 7 + 7 =$	x	inverse
10. $3(5 + 2) = 3 \times 5 + 3 \times 2$	21	distributive
11. $a(b + c) = a \cdot b + a \cdot c$	$a \cdot c + a \cdot b$	distributive
12. $a \cdot \frac{1}{a} =$	a	recripocal

Chapter 2: Review of Properties of Numbers (cont.)

Summary of Properties of Numbers

Numbers operations have certain properties or rules. The properties related to algebra include the Identity Properties, Commutative Properties, and Associative Properties of Addition and Multiplication, and the Distributive Property of Multiplication Over Addition.

Identity Property of Addition	$a + 0 = a$
Identity Property of Multiplication	$b \cdot 1 = b$
Commutative Property of Addition	$a + b = b + a$
Commutative Property of Multiplication	$a \cdot b = b \cdot a$
Associative Property of Addition	$(a + b) + c = a + (b + c)$
Associative Property of Multiplication	$(a \cdot b) \cdot c = a \cdot (b \cdot c)$
Inverse Operations	Addition and Subtraction Multiplication and Division
Reciprocal or Multiplicative Inverse Property	$a \cdot \dfrac{1}{a} = 1$
Distributive Property	$a(b + c) = a \cdot b + a \cdot c$

Tips to Remember

- Zero plus any number is that number, so it identifies the original number.

    $2{,}567 + 0 = 2{,}567$ $a + 0 = a$

- Any number multiplied by one identifies the original number.

    $45{,}987 \times 1 = 45{,}987$ $c \cdot 1 = c$

- Addition and multiplication have commutative properties because it does not matter the order in which you add or multiply the numbers. In subtraction and division, the order of the numbers makes a difference in the answers, so subtraction and division do not have commutative properties.

Chapter 2: Review of Properties of Numbers (cont.)

- Addition and multiplication have associative properties because it does not matter how you group the numbers, the answer is the same.

- Distributive property of multiplication over addition in expressions such as $4(a + 5a)$, multiply and then add.

Real Life Applications of Properties of Numbers

Properties of numbers are used in accounting, finding velocity, chemistry, finding profits, finding times in different time zones, and art.

Chapter 3: Exponents and Exponential Expressions

Introduction to Exponents and Exponential Expressions

Many times in working with mathematics, we need to multiply the same number by itself many times. For example, when bacteria double each hour, think about how many bacteria you have after 13 hours—starting with one bacteria.

$$2 \times 2 \times 2 \times 2 \times 2 \times 2 \times 2 \times 2 \times 2 \times 2 \times 2 \times 2 \times 2$$

Rather than writing out the repeated multiplication, symbols called **exponents** can be used as shorthand notation to indicate the action of repeated multiplication. The number repeated as multiplication above can be written as 2^{13}. In this section, we will be looking at how exponents are used, how to evaluate expressions using exponents, and discovering what rules are helpful in simplifying and evaluating exponential expressions.

Concepts of Exponents and Exponential Expressions

1. Whole Number Exponents
2. Negative Exponents
3. Fractional Exponents
4. Raising to the Zero Power
5. Raising a Power to a Power
6. Simplifying Exponential Expressions

Explanations of the Concepts of Exponents and Exponential Expressions

1 Whole Number Exponents

The **exponent** is the number indicating how many times the number is multiplied by itself. The **square** of a number means you multiply the number by itself. The **cube** of a number means that you multiply the number times itself three times. In the exponential expression 4^3, the 4 is the **root**, and the ^{3} is the **exponent**. 4^3 is the same as $4 \times 4 \times 4$. Since there are no parentheses, start at the left and move right $4 \times 4 = 16$, $16 \times 4 = 64$, so $4^3 = 64$.

Examples of Exponents:

The square of a number means you multiply the number by itself.
For example, 7^2 means 7 squared or 7 raised to the second power.
$7 \times 7 = 49$
So $7^2 = 49$.

Chapter 3: Exponents and Exponential Expressions (cont.)

Scientists use exponents in **scientific notation** when they are working with very large or very small numbers. This may be necessary when dealing with the vast distances of space or the tiny particles of an atom.

Examples:

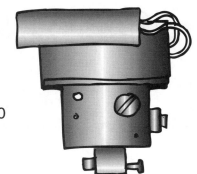

10^8 = 10 to the 8th power

This is 10 times itself 8 times or

$10 \times 10 \times 10 \times 10 \times 10 \times 10 \times 10 \times 10 = 100,000,000$

$10^8 = 100,000,000$

$5.06 \times 10^{15} = 5,060,000,000,000,000$

This number uses scientific notation to write a very large number.

Exponents are sometimes used in a combination of numbers and variables together, and these are called **algebraic expressions**. For example, $3x^5$, $(5x^3y)^4$, and $(4 + x)^2$ are examples of algebraic expressions that use exponents. Many times we need to simplify these expressions as a part of solving equations and problems. To help in simplification, there are some simple rules that are useful.

Multiplication Rule

In general, $a^m \times a^n = a^{m+n}$. In words, if multiplying exponential expressions with the same base, add the exponents and keep the same base.

Example of Multiplying Exponential Expressions With Coefficients:

Problem: $(3x^2)(5x^5) =$

Step 1: Multiply the coefficients $(3)(5) = 15$

Step 2: Add the exponents $2 + 5 = 7$

Step 3: Combine the terms $15x^7$

Answer: $(3x^2)(5x^5) = 15x^7$

Chapter 3: Exponents and Exponential Expressions (cont.)

Division Rule

In general, $a^m \div a^n = a^{m-n}$. In words, if dividing exponential expressions with the same base, subtract the exponents and keep the same base.

Example of Dividing Expressions With the Same Base:

Problem: Suppose we need to simplify the expression, $a^5 \div a^2$.

Step 1: To investigate, let's think of the division in fraction form, $\dfrac{a^5}{a^2}$

This should be simple to do using the definition of an exponent.

What does a^5 mean? $a \times a \times a \times a \times a$

What does a^2 mean? $a \times a$

That means that $\dfrac{a^5}{a^2} = \dfrac{a \times a \times a \times \cancel{a} \times \cancel{a}}{\cancel{a} \times \cancel{a}} = a \times a \times a$

Step 2: Consider the exponents 5 and 2: What was the new simplified exponent? 3

How do we get 3 from 5 and 2? SUBTRACT

Answer: $a^5 \div a^2 = a^3$

Dividing Exponential Expressions

To divide exponential expressions with the same root or base, subtract the exponents and put the answer with the root or base number. For example, for $4^5 \div 4^2 =$, the root or base is 4. The exponents are ^{5} and ^{2}. Subtract the exponents $^{5-2=3}$. Put the answer with the root 4^3, so $4^5 \div 4^2 = 4^3$.

You can divide exponential expressions with coefficients if they have the same base or root. Divide the coefficients, subtract the exponents, and combine the terms. For example, in $4d^6 \div 2d^2$, the exponents are ^{6} and ^{2}. Subtract the exponents $^{6-2=4}$. Divide the coefficients $4 \div 2 = 2$. Put the answers for the exponent and the coefficients with the root, $2d^4$, so $4d^6 \div 2d^2 = 2d^4$.

Examples of Dividing Exponential Expressions:

Problem: $8^5 \div 8^2 =$

Step 1: Subtract the exponents. $^{5-2=3}$

Step 2: Put the exponent with the base and raise to the power. $8^3 = 512$

Answer: $8^5 \div 8^2 = 512$

Problem: $\dfrac{6x^2}{6x^3}$

Step 1: Subtract the exponents. x^{2-3}

Step 2: Note that $6 \div 6 = 1$, so x^{-1} is the simplified answer.

Answer: $\dfrac{6x^2}{6x^3} = x^{-1}$

Problem: $x^4 \div x^{(-4)}$

Step 1: Subtract the exponents. $4-(-4)=8$

Step 2: Put the new exponent with the base. x^8

Answer: $x^4 \div x^{(-4)} = x^8$

Problem: $8b^{-4} \div 2b^2$

Step 1: Divide the coefficients. $8 \div 2 = 4$

Step 2: Subtract the exponents. $-4-2=-6$

Step 3: Put the new exponent with the new coefficient and base. $4b^{-6}$

Answer: $8b^{-4} \div 2b^2 = 4b^{-6}$

In the last example, the base is raised to a negative exponent. How should this be interpreted? As b times itself negative 6 times?

② Negative Exponents

To solve problems with negative exponents, find the reciprocal of a number. When you find the reciprocal of a number, you make the numerator the denominator and the denominator the numerator.

Examples of Reciprocals:

$\frac{1}{2}$ reciprocal is $\frac{2}{1}$ 3 reciprocal is $\frac{1}{3}$ $\dfrac{a}{b}$ reciprocal is $\dfrac{b}{a}$

Change the negative exponents to reciprocals by taking the reciprocal of the number that is raised to a power and change the exponent to a positive number.

Examples of Solving Problems With Negative Exponents:

Problem: 5^{-2}

Step 1: Find the reciprocal of the number that is raised to a power.

Chapter 3: Exponents and Exponential Expressions (cont.)

$5 = \frac{5}{1}$ The reciprocal of $\frac{5}{1}$ is $\frac{1}{5}$.

Step 2: Change the exponent in the reciprocal to a positive number. $\frac{1}{5^2}$

Step 3: Find the final **answer.** $5^{-2} = \frac{1}{5^2} = \frac{1}{25}$

Problem: x^{-4}

Step 1: Find the reciprocal of the number that is raised to a power.

$x = \frac{x}{1}$ The reciprocal is $\frac{1}{x}$.

Step 2: Change the exponent in the reciprocal to a positive number. $\frac{1}{x^4}$

Step 3: Find the final **answer.** $x^{-4} = \frac{1}{x^4}$

③ Fractional Exponents

Fractional exponents can be changed into radical expressions. The numerator is the exponent of the number under the radical sign, and the denominator is the index.

Example of Fractional Exponents as Radical Expressions:

Problem: $y^{\frac{2}{3}} =$

Step 1: Write the base under the radical. $\sqrt{y}$

Step 2: Raise the base the power of the numerator. $\sqrt{y^2}$

Step 3: Put the denominator as the index. $\sqrt[3]{y^2}$

Answer: $y^{\frac{2}{3}} = \sqrt[3]{y^2}$

④ Raising to the Zero Power

If we can have any number as an exponent, what does 2^0 mean? Let's try to use our earlier understanding to see what the answer should be. Suppose we start with $\frac{2^4}{2^4}$. We know that any number divided by itself is 1. So, we know that $\frac{2^4}{2^4} = 1$. The rule for dividing exponential expressions with the same base says that you simplify by subtracting exponents to get the new exponent. That would mean that $\frac{2^4}{2^4} = 2^{4-4}$. This tells us that $\frac{2^4}{2^4} = 1$ and $\frac{2^4}{2^4} = 2^0$. This has to mean that $2^0 = 1$.

In general, $a^0 = 1$. In words, any base raised to the zero power is 1.

Chapter 3: Exponents and Exponential Expressions (cont.)

5 Raising a Power to a Power

Consider how to handle $(3^3)^2$. We want to raise a power to another power. If the definition of an exponent is used, we can investigate how this should work. Consider the meaning of 3^3. $3^3 = 3 \times 3 \times 3$. This gives the result that $(3^3)^2 = (3 \times 3 \times 3)^2$. Raising the inside to the second power would mean to take what is inside the parentheses and multiply it by itself, so $(3^3)^2 = (3 \times 3 \times 3)^2 = (3 \times 3 \times 3)(3 \times 3 \times 3) = 3 \times 3 \times 3 \times 3 \times 3 \times 3 = 3^6$. Consider the exponents 3 and 2. What was the new simplified exponent? 6. How do we get 6 from 3 and 2? MULTIPLY.

Power to a Power Rule

In general, $(a^m)^n = a^{m \cdot n}$. In words, to raise a power to a power, multiply the exponents.

Examples of Raising the Exponential Power:

Problem: $(2^2)^5$

Step 1: Multiply the exponents. $2 \times 5 = 10$

Step 2: Raise the base to the power. $2^{10} = 1,024$

Answer: $(2^2)^5 = 1,024$

Problem: $(5^5)^0$

Step 1: Multiply the exponents. $5 \times 0 = 0$

Remember 0 times any number is 0.

Step 2: Raise the base to the power. $5^0 = 1$

Any number to the zero power is 1.

Answer: $(5^5)^0 = 1$

6 Evaluating Exponential Expressions

To evaluate exponential expressions, compute the value of the exponential expression as it falls according to the order of operations rules.

Examples of Multiplying Exponential Expressions:

Problem: $4(5)^2$

Step 1: First compute the value of the exponential expression.

$(5)^2 = (5 \times 5) = 25$

Chapter 3: Exponents and Exponential Expressions (cont.)

Step 2: Then multiply by the coefficient. $4 \times (25)$

Answer: $4(5)^2 = 100$.

Problem: $6(7 - 3)^2 =$

Step 1: First do what is in the parentheses.

   $7 - 3 = 4$ Which makes the problem $6(4)^2 =$

Step 2: Compute the value of the exponential expression. $6(4 \times 4)$

Step 3: Then multiply by the coefficient. $6(16) = 96$

Answer: $6(7 - 3)^2 = 96$.

Adding and Subtracting Exponential Expressions

Exponential expressions can be added or subtracted if they have exactly the same base and exactly the same exponent by adding or subtracting the coefficients. When the variable parts match exactly, we call these like terms.

Examples of Adding and Subtracting Exponential Expressions:

Problem: $4(y^3) + 8(y^3)$

The bases, y, are exactly the same, and the exponent, ^{3}, is exactly the same, so the like terms can be added. Notice how this is like asking the sum of 4 apples + 8 apples.

Step 1: Add the coefficients: $4 + 8 = 12$

Answer: $4(y^3) + 8(y^3) = 12y^3$

Problem: $8(v^7) - 4(v^7)$

The bases, v, are the same, and the exponent, ^{7}, is the same, so they can be subtracted.

Step 1: Subtract the coefficients: $8 - 4 = 4$

Answer: $8(v^7) - 4(v^7) = 4v^7$

$$7(x^3) + 4(x^3)$$
$$3(y^2) \quad 9(v^5) + 8(v^5)$$
$$- \quad 2(y^2)$$

Name: *Connie Dvorak*   Date: *Some time*

Chapter 3: Exponents and Exponential Expressions (cont.)

Practice: Exponents and Exponential Power

Directions: Solve and show your work.

Evaluate each exponential expression.

1. 10^2 $10 \cdot 10 = 100$

2. 6^{10} $6 \cdot 6 \cdot 6 \cdot 6 \cdot 6 \cdot 6 \cdot 6 \cdot 6 \cdot 6 \cdot 6 = 1009000$

3. y^0 $y \cdot 0 = 0$

Evaluate exponential expressions with coefficients.

4. $5(-3)^3$ 45

5. $10(b)^2$ $(b \cdot b) \cdot 10$

Add and subtract exponential expressions with like terms.

6. $10(z^3) + 2(z^3)$ $12 \cdot z^6$

7. $5(z^3) - 3(z^3)$ $2 \cdot z^6$

8. $3(z^3) - 1(z)$ $2 \cdot z^4$

Multiply exponential expressions.

9. $(z^3)(z^4)$ z^7

10. $(c^3)(c^2)$ c^5

Name: _____ Date: _____

Chapter 3: Exponents and Exponential Expressions (cont.)

11. $(6x^4)(3x^2)$ _____ $9x^6$ _____

Divide exponential expressions.

12. $3^2 \div 3$ _____ 3 _____

13. $x^4 \div x^2$ _____ x^2 _____

14. $\dfrac{5^2}{1^3}$ _____ 8.33 _____

Raise to the power indicated.

15. $(7^2)^0$ _____ 0 _____

16. $(x^4)^2$ _____ $(x^4)^2$ _____

17. $(5y^3)^3$ _____ $(5y^3)^3$ _____

Change the negative exponents to positive exponents.

18. 5^{-4} _____ $\frac{1}{5}\,4$ _____

19. 2^{-6} _____ $\frac{1}{2}\,6$ _____

20. $\left(\dfrac{1}{a}\right)^{-3}$ _____ a^3 _____

Chapter 3: Exponents and Exponential Expressions (cont.)

Summary of Exponents and Exponential Expressions

The exponent is the number indicating how many times the number is multiplied by itself. The square of a number means you multiply the number by itself. The cube of a number means that you multiply the number times itself three times.

Tips to Remember

- Multiplying Exponential Expressions With the Same Base: Add the exponents and keep the same base.

- Dividing Exponential Expressions by the Same Base: Subtract the exponents and keep the base.

- Negative Exponential Expressions: Find the reciprocal and change the exponent to a positive.

- Any base raised to the zero power is 1.

- Raising a Power to a Power: Multiply the exponents.

Real Life Applications of Exponents

Exponents are used in scientific notation as shorthand for very large numbers. Instead of writing 6,000,000,000, scientists write 6×10^9. Another use for exponents is for finding the surface area of a room that needs to be painted to determine how much paint is needed. Construction workers use exponents to determine the number of 2 x 4s needed so they can estimate the costs of construction.

Chapter 4: Roots and Radicals

Introduction to the Concepts of Roots and Radicals

Exponents and roots go together because they turn out to be inverse operations. What one action does, the opposite action undoes. So raising a quantity to the 2nd power is undone by finding the square root. In the previous sections, inverse operations were introduced. The inverse of addition is subtraction, and the inverse of multiplication is division. This section focuses on the most common roots and radicals and how to interpret, evaluate, and simplify algebraic expressions that include roots and radicals.

Concepts of Roots and Radicals

1 Square Roots and Perfect Squares

2 Cube Roots and Higher

3 Negative Radicands

4 Simplifying Radical Expressions

Explanations of Roots and Radicals

1 Square Roots and Perfect Squares

A square root of a number is found by finding out what number, multiplied by itself, equals that given number. What number, multiplied by itself, equals 36? The answer is 6 because 6 × 6 = 36. Using an exponent, you could write $6^2 = 36$. The root number in this example is 6. A radical sign $\sqrt{\ }$ is used as a symbol to mean that you need to find the square root. The question, "what number multiplied by itself equals 36," can be written symbolically as $\sqrt{36}$. You can check your answer by multiplying the number times itself.

Some numbers are **perfect squares**. That means that the square root of that number is a whole number. 100, 25, 16, and 9 are all perfect squares because each has a square root that is a whole number. ($\sqrt{100} = 10$, $\sqrt{25} = 5$, $\sqrt{16} = 4$ and $\sqrt{9} = 3$).

Every number has two square roots—a positive square root and a negative square root. This is because when two negative numbers are multiplied together, their product or answer is a positive number. For example: $-4 \times -4 = 16$ and $4 \times 4 = 16$. So is $\sqrt{16}$, (the square root of 16), 4 or -4? A radical sign $\sqrt{\ }$ is used as a symbol to mean "find the principal or positive square root." This means that $\sqrt{16} = 4$.

Numbers such as 3 are not perfect squares because the square root is not a whole number. The symbol ≈ means "is approximately" and is used because the number has been rounded off to provide an estimate of the exact root value. The square root of 3 or $\sqrt{3} \approx$ 1.732; however, if you multiply 1.732 times 1.732 the answer is 2.999824. If the square root is approximated by rounding to the nearest thousandths, it would be 3.000.

Chapter 4: Roots and Radicals (cont.)

Examples of Square Roots:

$\sqrt{81} =$ or the square root of 81 =
What number times itself = 81?
$9 \times 9 = 81$
Therefore, $\sqrt{81} = 9$

The above example was a perfect square. If the number is not a perfect square, then the square root is not a whole number.

Example of a Number That Is Not a Perfect Square:

$\sqrt{7} \approx 2.646$
$2.646 \times 2.646 = 7.001316$
Rounded to the nearest hundredth 7.001316 = 7.00

2 Cubed Roots and Higher

Numbers can also have exponents other than 2. When a small three is written to the right of the number (n^3), the number is multiplied by itself 3 times. This number then is called cubed or raised to the 3rd power. When 3 is cubed or taken to the 3rd power, it is written as 3^3. Multiply $3 \times 3 \times 3$ to get 27, so three cubed (3^3) = 27. Scientific notation uses powers of 10 (n^{10}) for example. They would write the number 1,000,000 like this: 1×10^6 or 1 times $10 \times 10 \times 10 \times 10 \times 10 \times 10$.

Cubed roots can also be found by asking "what number times itself three times is the number in question?". The sign for finding the cubed roots is $\sqrt[3]{}$. The cube root of 64 written as $\sqrt[3]{64}$ becomes what number multiplied by itself 3 times = 64? $4 \times 4 \times 4 = 64$. Remember that the number in the radical sign, in this case 3, is the index, and the number under the radical sign is the radicand. In this case, the radicand is 64.

The index can be a number greater than two or three, for example $\sqrt[4]{16}$. The index is 4, so what number times itself four times equals 16? $\sqrt[4]{16} = 2$ because $2 \times 2 \times 2 \times 2 = 16$. Notice that $2^4 = 16$.

Examples of Cubed Roots and Higher:

$\sqrt[3]{n}$ is the sign for finding a cubed root.

$\sqrt[3]{64} =$

What number times itself three times equals 64?

$4 \times 4 = 16$ and $16 \times 4 = 64$, so $4 \times 4 \times 4 = 64$

4 multiplied by itself 3 times = 64.

$\sqrt[3]{64} = 4$

Chapter 4: Roots and Radicals (cont.)

The notation $\sqrt[x]{n}$ can be used with any index number.

$\sqrt[6]{64}$

The question is "What number multiplied by itself six times equals 64?".
Starting from the left and moving right, since there are no parentheses:

2 x 2 = 4, 4 x 2 = 8, 8 x 2 = 16, 16 x 2 = 32, 32 x 2 = 64

2 x 2 x 2 x 2 x 2 x 2 = 64

$\sqrt[6]{64}$ = 2 because 2 times itself 6 times = 64.

3 Negative Radicands

When there are negative radicands, the sign on the root number of the solution is determined by whether the index is odd or even. The index in this radical, $\sqrt[x]{n}$, is x, and the radicand is n. If the index is an even number, you cannot compute the value. If the index is odd and the radicand is a negative number, the root is a negative number. Radical expressions with negative radicands can only be solved if the index is an odd number.

Examples of Radical Expressions With Negative Radicands That Can Be Solved:

$\sqrt[3]{-8}$ = -2 because -2 x -2 x -2 = -8

$\sqrt[5]{-32}$ = -2 because -2 x -2 x -2 x -2 x -2 = -32

Example of a Radical Expression With a Negative Radicand That Cannot Be Solved:

$\sqrt[4]{-16}$ The index is even, so it cannot be solved.
2 x 2 x 2 x 2 = 16 and -2 x -2 x -2 x -2 = 16
There is no solution that equals -16.

Chapter 4: Roots and Radicals (cont.)

4 Simplifying Radical Expressions

Rules for Simplifying Radical Expressions

- In simplifying radical expressions: If two numbers are multiplied under the radical sign, you may separate the two expressions. Find the square roots of each one and multiply the solutions together.

- If two radical expressions are multiplied together, they can be written as a single product under the same radical sign.

- You may also find factors for the number under the radical and take the root of the factors.

- If two numbers are divided under a radical sign, they can be separated into two radicals.

- Multiplying the numerator and denominator of a radical expression by the same number does not change the value.

- Radical expressions can be added and subtracted if each index is the same and each number under the radical sign is the same.

- Radical expressions can be written as fractional exponents. The numerator is the power of the number under the radical sign; the denominator is the number that is the index.

- Fractional exponents can be changed into radical expressions. The numerator is the exponent of the number under the radical sign, and the denominator is the index.

- Radical Expressions are not simplified if there is a radical in the denominator.

Examples of the Rules for Simplifying Radical Expressions:

- If two numbers are multiplied under the radical sign, you may separate the two expressions.

Problem: $\sqrt{(4)(9)}$

Step 1: Separate the two expressions. $(\sqrt{4})(\sqrt{9})$

Step 2: Find the square roots of each factor. $\sqrt{4} = 2 \qquad \sqrt{9} = 3$

Step 3: Multiply the solutions. $(2)(3) = 6$

Answer: $\sqrt{(4)(9)} = 6$

Chapter 4: Roots and Radicals (cont.)

- If two radical expressions are multiplied together, they can be written as products under the same radical sign.

Problem: $(\sqrt{3})(\sqrt{27}) =$

Step 1: Write as products under the same radical sign. $\sqrt{(3)(27)} =$

Step 2: Multiply the numbers under the radical. $3 \times 27 = 81$

Step 3: $\sqrt{81}$ The square root of 81 = 9.

Answer: $(\sqrt{3})(\sqrt{27}) = 9$

- Find factors for the number under the radical and take the square root of the factors.

Problem: $\sqrt{18}$

Step 1: Find the factors of 18. 2×9 or 3×6

Step 2: 9 is a perfect square so put the 2×9 under the radical sign. $\sqrt{(2)(9)}$

Step 3: Remember that parentheses mean to multiply the numbers.

$$\sqrt{(2)(9)} = (\sqrt{2})(\sqrt{9})$$

Step 4: $\sqrt{9} = 3$

$$\sqrt{(2)(9)} = 3\sqrt{2}$$

Step 5: The square root of 2 is not a whole number. Rounding it to the nearest thousandth, it is ≈ 1.414

Step 6: $\sqrt{(2)(9)} \approx 3 \times 1.414$. Note that this is $\approx$ not = because the number has been rounded.

Answer: $\sqrt{(2)(9)} \approx 4.242$

- If two numbers are divided under a radical sign, they can be separated into two radicals.

Problem: $\sqrt{\dfrac{9}{4}}$

Step 1: Put the numbers under two radical signs. $\dfrac{\sqrt{9}}{\sqrt{4}}$

Step 2: Find the square roots. $\sqrt{9} = 3$ $\sqrt{4} = 2$

Answer: $\sqrt{\dfrac{9}{4}} = \dfrac{3}{2} = 1\dfrac{1}{2}$

Chapter 4: Roots and Radicals (cont.)

- Example of multiplying the numerator and denominator of a radical expression by the same number and not changing the value:

Problem: $\dfrac{5}{\sqrt{3}} =$

Step 1: Construct a fraction with the radical as the numerator and denominator.

$$\dfrac{5}{\sqrt{3}}\left(\dfrac{\sqrt{3}}{\sqrt{3}}\right)=$$

Remember that a number divided by itself is equal to 1, so the value will not change.

Step 2: Multiply the expression by the fraction. Put the two square roots in the denominator under the same radical.

$$\dfrac{5}{\sqrt{3}}\left(\dfrac{\sqrt{3}}{\sqrt{3}}\right) = \dfrac{5\sqrt{3}}{\sqrt{3(3)}} = \dfrac{5\sqrt{3}}{\sqrt{9}}$$

Step 3: Find the square root of the denominator.

Answer: $\dfrac{5}{\sqrt{3}} = \dfrac{5\sqrt{3}}{\sqrt{9}} = \dfrac{5\sqrt{3}}{3}$

- Radical expressions can be added and subtracted if each index is the same and each number under the radical sign is the same.

Example Addition and Subtraction of Radicals:

Problem: $3\sqrt{4} + 4\sqrt{4} =$

Step 1: Add the coefficients: $3 + 4 = 7$

Step 2: Bring the radical over.

Answer: $3\sqrt{4} + 4\sqrt{4} = 7\sqrt{4}$

Chapter 4: Roots and Radicals (cont.)

Problem: $2\sqrt[3]{27} + \sqrt[3]{27} =$

Both have the same index and radicand.

Step 1: Add the coefficients: $2 + 1$

Step 2: Bring the radical over.

Answer: $2\sqrt[3]{27} + \sqrt[3]{27} = 3\sqrt[3]{27}$

Problem: $3\sqrt[3]{x} - \sqrt[3]{x} =$

Both have the same index and radicand.

Step 1: Subtract the coefficients: $3 - 1$

Step 2: Bring the radical over.

Answer: $3\sqrt[3]{x} - \sqrt[3]{x} = 2\sqrt[3]{x}$

- Radical expressions can be written as fractional exponents. The numerator is the power of the number under the radical sign, and the denominator is the number that is the index.

Example of Radical Expression as Fractional Exponent:

Problem: $\sqrt[4]{x^3}$

Index = 4   Exponent = 3

Step 1: Copy the base under the radical sign. x

Step 2: Make the new exponent a fraction. The old exponent becomes the numerator, and the index becomes the denominator. $\frac{3}{4}$

Answer: $\sqrt[4]{x^3} = x^{\frac{3}{4}}$

- Fractional exponents can be changed into radical expressions. The numerator is the exponent of the number under the radical sign, and the denominator is the index.

Example of Fractional Exponents as Radical Expressions:

Problem: $y^{\frac{2}{3}} =$

Step 1: Write the base under the radical. $\sqrt{y}$

Step 2: Raise the base the power of the numerator. $\sqrt{y^2}$

Step 3: Put the denominator as the index. $\sqrt[3]{y^2}$

Answer: $y^{\frac{2}{3}} = \sqrt[3]{y^2}$

Name: _____ Date: _____

Chapter 4: Roots and Radicals (cont.)

Practice: Roots and Radical Expressions

Directions: Solve and show your work.

Find the square roots and identify which ones are perfect square roots.

1. $\sqrt{4}$ _____   **2.** $\sqrt{9}$ _____   **3.** $\sqrt{1}$ _____

4. $\sqrt{3}$ _____   **5.** $\sqrt{2}$ _____

Solve using two radical signs.

6. $\sqrt{(25)(9)}$ _____   **7.** $\sqrt{(4)(16)}$ _____

8. $\sqrt{16y^2}$ $y > 0$ _____

Solve by multiplying radicals.

9. $(\sqrt{y})(\sqrt{y})$ $y > 0$ _____   **10.** $(\sqrt{3})(\sqrt{12})$ _____

Solve by factoring.

11. $\sqrt{32}$ _____   **12.** $\sqrt{125}$ _____

Simplify by dividing radicals. Remember: a radical is not simplified if it has a radical in the denominator.

13. $\sqrt{\dfrac{25}{36}}$ _____   **14.** $\sqrt{\dfrac{64}{16}}$ _____   **15.** $\sqrt{\dfrac{4}{3}}$ _____

Name: _____ Date: _____

Chapter 4: Roots and Radicals (cont.)

Simplify by adding and subtracting radicals.

16. $3\sqrt{36} + \sqrt{1}$ _____

17. $4\sqrt[5]{x} + 5\sqrt[5]{x}$ _____

18. $6\sqrt[5]{x} + \sqrt[2]{x}$ _____

19. $8\sqrt{5} - 4\sqrt{5}$ _____

20. $9\sqrt{2y} - 3\sqrt{2y}$ _____

Find the cube roots and higher.

21. $\sqrt[3]{8}$ _____

22. $\sqrt[3]{27}$ _____

23. $\sqrt[6]{64}$ _____

24. $\sqrt[9]{1}$ _____

Solve these problems with negative radicands if possible.

25. $\sqrt[4]{-81}$ _____

26. $\sqrt[3]{-1}$ _____

27. $\sqrt{-4}$ _____

Write as fractional exponents.

28. $\sqrt[5]{a^2}$ _____

29. $\sqrt{7}$ _____

Write as radical expressions.

30. $b^{\frac{2}{3}}$ _____

31. $(5y)^{\frac{1}{3}}$ _____

32. $10^{\frac{1}{2}}$ _____

Chapter 4: Roots and Radicals (cont.)

Summary of Roots and Radicals

A square number is the result when any positive integer is squared. For example, 16 is a square number because it is the result of 4^2. The exponent tells how many times the number is multiplied by itself. Square roots are found by finding out what number taken times itself equals the number in question. A radical sign $\sqrt{n}$ is used as a symbol for the square root of a number that is represented by the variable n. You can also find cube roots and higher roots. Finding the cube root is written as $\sqrt[3]{n}$. The question is "what number multiplied by itself 3 times will equal n?". Higher roots will be represented by $\sqrt[x]{n}$ where x is the variable representing the index of the root and n is the radicand for which you are finding the root.

Tips to Remember

- Square Root: What number times itself equals the number?

- Perfect Squares: The root is a whole number.

- Cube Roots: What number times itself three times equals the number?

- $\sqrt[n]{729}$ Higher than cubed roots: The index in the radical tells how many times the radicand has been raised. The question becomes "What number times itself n times equals 729?".

- To simplify radical expressions, use the property rules and rules of operations.

Real Life Applications of Roots

Squares and square roots are used in finding the surface area of a square or length of sides. If you know the surface area of the square, that could help find out how much paint is needed for a certain area. Skydivers use radical equations to find the velocity of freefalling using the formula $v = \sqrt{2gd}$.

Chapter 5: Operations on Algebraic Expressions

Introduction to Operations on Algebraic Expressions

According to the NCTM Standards, students need to be able to:
- Understand meanings of operations and how they relate to one another.
- Compute fluently and make reasonable estimates. NCTM.

Algebra uses numbers, symbols, and letters. This section describes the operations on algebraic expressions. An expression is a certain number or variable, or numbers and variables, combined by operations such as addition, subtraction, multiplication, or division. Different symbols, shown in the table in the beginning of the worktext, mean different things. All symbols help describe the operations to be done. The letters, or variables, represent an unknown number or quantity.

Concepts of Operations on Algebraic Expressions

1. Operating on Algebraic Expressions
2. Absolute Value
3. The Operation of Addition on Algebraic Expressions
4. The Operation of Subtraction on Algebraic Expressions
5. The Operation of Multiplication on Algebraic Expressions
6. The Operation of Division on Algebraic Expressions
7. The Operations of Adding, Subtracting, and Multiplying by Zero
8. Algebraic Expressions Order of Operations
9. Operating on Signed Numbers

Explanations of Concepts of Operations on Algebraic Expressions

1 Operating on Algebraic Expressions

As stated above, an **expression** is a certain number or variable, or numbers and variables, combined by operations such as addition, subtraction, multiplication, or division. There are monomial and polynomial algebraic expressions. **Monomial expressions** are of the form ax^n, where a is any real number, and the exponent n is a positive integer. 14, x, and $-6x^2y$ are monomial expressions. **Polynomial expressions** are a sum of monomial expressions. An

Chapter 5: Operations on Algebraic Expressions (cont.)

example of a polynomial expression is $x^2 + (-4x) + (-5)$. Special kinds of polynomial expressions are binomial and trinomial expressions. **Binomials** are the sum of two monomials, for example $2x - 9$ or $2ab + b^2$. **Trinomial expressions** are the sum of three monomial terms, for example $x^2 - 5x - 3$ or $a^2 + 3ab - 5b^2$. This section examines the operations performed on algebraic expressions.

Remember that mathematics has four basic operations that can be performed: addition, subtraction, multiplication, and division. The operations listed are used to act on terms. A term can be a number (like 6), it can be a variable (like m), or it can be a product or quotient of numbers and variables (like $6m$ or $\frac{7m}{8y}$). At times we will need to know if terms can be called like terms. For example, $12xy$ and $-7xy$ are **like terms** because their variable parts are exactly alike. An example of terms that are **unlike** would be $12xy$ and $-7x^2y$. The variables used are the same (x's and y's), but in one term the x is raised to the second power—this causes the terms to be unlike. In a term that combines numbers and variables, like the monomial $4a$, the number 4 is called the **coefficient**. In the term $12xy$, the coefficient would be 12. Determining like terms and unlike terms and the meaning of the coefficient is important in being able to work with numbers, variables, and operations.

Symbols are used to indicate what operation is to be used in solving the problem.

+ sign indicates addition.

− sign indicates subtraction.

÷, /, or $\sqrt{}$ signs indicate division.

×, ( ), or • signs indicate multiplication.

The operations are performed on numbers and variables. Numbers were discussed in the first section of this worktext. As a review, the number line for the whole numbers starts at zero and uses equally spaced marks to represent 1, 2, 3, and the other numbers that belong to the infinite set of whole numbers.

Whole Number Line
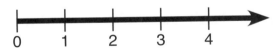

The set of whole numbers was expanded to form a new set of numbers, called the integers. The integer number line expands the whole numbers to the left from zero. Mathematically, we say that each whole number n has an opposite or inverse on the number line, $-n$. We can define the set of integers as $\{\ldots, -3, -2, -1, 0, 1, 2, 3, \ldots\}$ and can illustrate it using a number line.

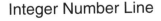
Integer Number Line

Chapter 5: Operations on Algebraic Expressions (cont.)

The positive integers will be those to the right of zero on the number line. The set of positive integers is {1, 2, 3, …}. The negative integers are those to the left of zero on the number line. The set of negative integers is {-1, -2, -3, …}. Notice that the number zero is not positive or negative. We can think of zero as neutral, as the buffer that separates the negative and positive integers.

② Absolute Value

The absolute value of a number n is the answer to the question "how far from zero is n on the number line?". For example, the absolute value of 7, shown symbolically as |7|, would be 7. The absolute value of |-7| is also 7. Examine the number line below. The distance from 0 to 7 is 7 marks and from 0 to -7 is also 7 marks.

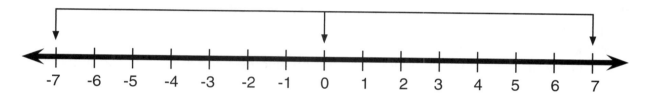

In general if the number is positive, then the absolute value is the number itself. If it is a negative number, the absolute value is the additive inverse or opposite of that number. The absolute value of a quantity is always positive or 0 because it represents a distance.

③ The Operation of Addition on Algebraic Expressions

When doing addition, only add like terms. When you add terms where the variables are the same, you add the coefficients or the numbers in front of the variable.

Examples of Adding Like Terms:

$3x + 6x$

Examples of Adding Coefficients:

A coefficient is a number to the left of the variable that is the multiplier of a variable or number usually written next to a variable. (Note: If the variables are the same in each equation, they are like terms.)

$3x + 6x = 9x$ $\frac{1}{3}a + 4a + 7a = 11\frac{1}{3}a$

$y + 2y = 3y$ (The coefficient of the first y is 1.)

     46

Chapter 5: Operations on Algebraic Expressions (cont.)

Unlike terms cannot be added if they include a number and letter, or two or more different variables.

> ### Example of an Algebraic Equation With Unlike Terms That Cannot Be Added:

$$5x + 3y + 2z$$

Additive Inverse Property of Addition

The basic concept for dealing with integers or other signed numbers involves the idea of opposites. Each integer has an opposite as shown in the examples below.

Integer	Opposite
-17	17
10	-10

What happens if a number and its opposite are added together? The sum of an integer and its opposite integer will always be zero! This result is true for all integers and is called the **Additive Inverse Property of Addition**.

For every integer, *a,* there is a unique integer, *-a,* so that, $a + (-a) = 0$. The integer *-a* is called the additive inverse of *a.*

Addition of Integers

Adding integers becomes a simple process if we put together basic addition facts and the new property just presented. To add numbers like 3 and -5, a model using +'s and –'s can be used. The illustration below shows 3 + signs representing the 3 and 5 – signs representing the -5. As stated above, adding 1+ and 1– = 0, forming a neutral pair. If you pair the pluses and minuses there are 3 +'s and 3 –'s, which will form 0 by the additive inverse property with 2 –'s left unpaired. The -5 has more power than the 3, so the answer will be a negative number. Find the difference between the numbers and add the sign. $3 + (-5) = -2$.

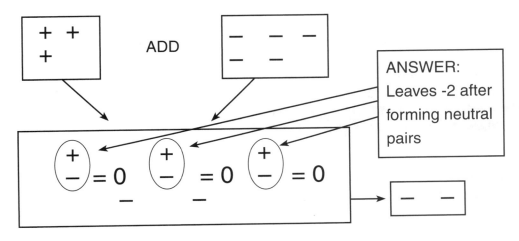

Chapter 5: Operations on Algebraic Expressions (cont.)

Example of Adding Two Integers With Different Signs:

Problem: -34 + 52 = ?

Step 1: Decide which of the addends will have more power, which has the greater absolute value. This determines if the answer is positive or negative.

Which addend, -34 or 52 has more power? In this case, the positive 52 has more power than the negative 34, so the answer will be positive. Note: $|52|$ = 52 and $|-32|$ = 32, so 52 has more power—it has the larger absolute value.

Step 2: Find the difference in the absolute values of the two numbers (treating both as positive quantities).

Find the difference between 52 and 34.

52 – 34 = 18.

Step 3: Take your answer from Step Two and attach the appropriate sign from Step One.

In Step One, we found that the answer would be positive. Add that sign to the answer.

Answer: So, -34 + 52 = 18.

Examples of Adding Integers With the Same Signs:

Both Positive: Add as always and get a positive answer.

17 + 76 = 93

Both Negative: Add as if they are both positive, and then attach a negative sign to your answer.

-17 + -76 = -93

4 The Operation of Subtraction on Algebraic Expressions

Only like terms can be subtracted. One number can be subtracted from another, and one variable can be subtracted from another if they are the same variable.

Example of Subtraction of Like Terms:

$6x - 2x = 4x$

Remember, unlike terms cannot be subtracted.

$5x - 5y$ (Cannot be solved because there are two different variables.)

Chapter 5: Operations on Algebraic Expressions (cont.)

Subtraction of Integers

When subtracting integers, connect what is known about the subtraction of whole numbers, basic subtraction facts, and take advantage of patterns seen.

Example of Subtracting Integers Both Positive:

8 – 3 = ?

When subtracting two positive integers, think about what the symbols ask you to do. We need to start with 8 +'s and from that set remove (subtract) 3 +'s and look to see what is left. We know that there are 5 +'s left. So, 8 – 3 = 5.

Example of Subtracting Negative Integers:

-8 – -3 = ?

When subtracting two negative integers, think about what the symbols ask you to do. We need to start with a set that has 8 -'s in it, and then remove (subtract) 3 -'s and look to see what is left. We know that there are 5 -'s left.
So, -8 – -3 = -5

Example of Subtracting Two Integers With One Positive and One Negative Sign:

-6 – 2 = ?
-6 – 2 = -8

Look at the symbols, start with 6 -'s, and then from that set remove 2 +'s. If the set only has -'s, where do we get the +'s to remove? Look at the problems in the table below, and see if there is a pattern that would help work with subtraction of integers of opposite signs.

Subtraction Problem	Answer	Addition Problem	Answer
6 – 2	4	6 + -2	4
-5 – 3	-8	-5 + -3	-8
7 – -2	9	7 + 2	9
-3 – -7	4	-3 + 7	4
47 – 23	24	47 + -23	24

Chapter 5: Operations on Algebraic Expressions (cont.)

1. Compare the subtraction problem to its partner addition problem. Each problem has the same solution.
2. How do the problems differ? Let's look at the first pair of problems.

Subtraction Problem	Answer	Addition Problem	Answer
6 − 2	4	6 + -2	4

- Both problems start with the same first number, 6.
- The two problems have different operations, subtraction versus addition.
- The subtraction problem has 2 as the second number. The addition problem has -2 (additive inverse of 2) as its second number.
- The answer is the same.

Does this pattern hold when comparing 47 − 23 = 24 and 47 + -23 = 24? Both of these problems have the same first number, 47. The problems have different operation signs, subtraction versus addition. In both problems the second numbers are additive inverses or opposites, 23 and -23. Are the answers the same? Yes. This pattern allows the replacement of any integer subtraction problem with an equivalent integer addition problem.

Integer Subtraction Rule

For all integers a and b
$$a - b = a + \text{-}b$$

Example:

-6 − 15 = ?
Think of the equivalent addition problem, -6 + -15 = ?
Since they are the same sign, add 6 and 15 to get 21 and attach a negative sign.
Since -6 + -15 = -21, we know -6 − 15 = -21.

5 **The Operation of Multiplication on Algebraic Expressions**

Any like or unlike terms can be multiplied. Numbers or variables (letters representing an unknown number) can be multiplied. A number times a variable or coefficients can be multiplied.

Examples of Multiplying Two Variables (or Two Unknown Numbers):

$a \bullet b = ab$ $y \bullet y = y^2$ (y squared)

Chapter 5: Operations on Algebraic Expressions (cont.)

Examples of Multiplying Numbers Times Variables:

$5 \cdot a = 5a$ $\qquad\qquad$ $8 \cdot b = 8b$

Examples of Multiplying Unlike Terms:

Multiply the coefficients together, and then put the variable at the end of the answer.

Problem:	$3 \cdot 6y =$
Step 1: Multiply the coefficients.	$3 \cdot 6 = 18$
Step 2: Put the variable at the end of the answer.	y
Answer:	$3 \cdot 6y = 18y$

Problem:	$2b \cdot 3 =$
Step 1: Multiply the coefficients.	$2 \cdot 3 = 6$
Step 2: Put the variable at the end of the answer.	b
Answer:	$2b \cdot 3 = 6b$

Examples of Multiplying Two Different Variables With Coefficients:

Multiply the coefficients first, and then multiply the variables and combine the two answers.

Problem:	$5a \cdot 4c =$
Step 1: Multiply the coefficients.	$5 \cdot 4 = 20$
Step 2: Multiply the variables.	$a \cdot c = ac$
Step 3: Put the variables at the end of the answer.	$20ac$
Answer:	$5a \cdot 4c = 20ac$

Problem:	$3z \cdot 5z =$
Step 1: Multiply the coefficients.	$3 \cdot 5 = 15$
Step 2: Multiply the variables.	$z \cdot z = z^2$
Step 3: Put the variables at the end of the answer.	$15z^2$
Answer:	$3z \cdot 5z = 15z^2$

Chapter 5: Operations on Algebraic Expressions (cont.)

Multiplication of Integers

Let's discuss the multiplication of integers using the problem 3×5. One way to think about 3×5, is as 3 groups with 5 objects in each group. So, multiplying two positive integers results in a positive integer answer, $3 \times 5 = 15$.

Multiplying Two Integers With Different Signs (one positive, one negative)

Using the same thinking with the multiplication problem, 3×-5, there would be 3 groups with 5 negatives in each. The figure then would show that the final answer is $-5 + -5 + -5 = -15$, or using multiplication, $3 \times -5 = -15$.

$$\boxed{\begin{matrix} - & - \\ - & - & - \end{matrix}} \quad \boxed{\begin{matrix} - & - \\ - & - & - \end{matrix}} \quad \boxed{\begin{matrix} - & - \\ - & - & - \end{matrix}}$$

$$-5 \quad + \quad -5 \quad + \quad -5 \quad = -15$$

Rule For Multiplying Two Integers With Different Signs

Multiply as if both were positive, and make the final answer negative.

Multiplying Two Negative Integers

Using what you know about multiplying integers, find the answer to -3×-5. Consider the examples below and look at the way the answers change—is there a pattern that sets up the obvious answer for -3×-5?

$3 \times -5 = -15$	Solution is in the illustration above.
$2 \times -5 = -10$	Apply the different sign rule for multiplication.
$1 \times -5 = -5$	Identity Property—any number multiplied by one is the number.
$0 \times -5 = 0$	Zero Property—any number multiplied by zero is zero.
$-1 \times -5 = 5$	Look at the pattern of answers, each changed by adding 5 to the previous answer, $-15 + 5 = -10$, $-10 + 5 = -5$, so -1×-5 must $= 5$.
$-2 \times -5 = 10$	Follow the pattern.
$-3 \times -5 = 15$	Note that the answer is positive, that $-3 \times -5 = 3 \times 5 = 15$.

Rule for Multiplying Two Negative Integers:

Multiply as if both were positive, and make the final answer positive.

Chapter 5: Operations on Algebraic Expressions (cont.)

6   The Operation of Division on Algebraic Expressions

Like and unlike terms can be divided and so can any two numbers or variables, or different variables. Phrases with numbers and variables can also be divided.

Examples of Dividing Any Two Numbers or Variables:

$$8 \div 4 = 2 \qquad\qquad x \div x = 1$$

Examples of Dividing Different Variables:

$$a \div b = \frac{a}{b}$$

Examples of Dividing Expressions With Numbers (Coefficients) and Variables:

Divide the coefficients, and then divide the variables. Multiply both answers together.

Problem:	$6a \div 2a =$
Step 1: Divide the coefficients.	$6 \div 2 = 3$
Step 2: Divide the variables.	$a \div a = 1$
Step 3: Multiply the answers of Step One and Two.	$3 \bullet 1 = 3$
Answer:	$6a \div 2a = 3$

Example of Dividing Two Different Variables:

Problem: $9ab \div 3a =$

Step 1: Divide the coefficients. $9 \div 3 = 3$

Step 2: Divide the variables. $ab \div a = \dfrac{ab}{a}$

since $\dfrac{a}{a} = 1$ then $1 \bullet b = b$

Step 3: Multiply the answers of

Steps One and Two. $3 \bullet b = 3b$

Answer: $9ab \div 3a = 3b$

Chapter 5: Operations on Algebraic Expressions (cont.)

Integer Division

Learning division is simply a matter of connecting division to multiplication. Since division and multiplication are inverse operations, integer division is built on what we already know. To answer the division problem, $15 \div 3$, most of us think of the associated multiplication problem, $3 \times$ what number $= 15$, and know that 5 is the solution.

The same thinking holds for integer division. Let's consider $-15 \div 3$ and outline the thinking process used to find the answer.

- Find: $-15 \div 3 = ?$
- Think: $3 \times$ what number $= -15$
- Know the basic fact: $3 \times 5 = 15$
- We want to end up with -15, not 15. We know the first factor, 3, is positive, so if -5 is the second factor, $3 \times -5 = -15$. A positive times a negative yields a negative answer.
- Found: $-15 \div 3 = -5$

This connection between multiplication and division allows us to "coast" using multiplication knowledge to find division answers.

7   The Operations of Adding, Subtracting, and Multiplying by Zero

When adding or subtracting zero and any number or variable, the answer is the number or variable. If you multiply a variable or number by zero, the answer is always zero. Zero divided by any number is zero, but numbers or variables cannot be divided by zero.

Examples of Adding and Subtracting Zero:

$2b + 0 = 2b$ $2b - 0 = 2b$

Examples of Multiplication by Zero:

$2a \bullet 0 = 0$ $-23 \times 0 = 0$

Examples of the Division of Zero by a Number or Variable:

$0 \div 4a = 0$ $0 \div (-6) = 0$

You cannot divide a number or variable by zero.

$4 \div 0 =$ cannot be divided $a \div 0 =$ cannot be divided

Name: _____ Date: _____

Practice: Operations on Algebraic Expressions

Directions: Perform the following operations. If you cannot perform the operation, explain why the operation cannot be done.

1. $335 + 1{,}567 =$ _____

2. $3a + 24b + 4c =$ _____

3. $\frac{1}{2}x + 5x =$ _____

4. $4x - 8y =$ _____

5. $7 - \frac{1}{2} =$ _____

6. $7y \bullet 8z =$ _____

7. $10a \bullet 35a =$ _____

8. $\frac{3}{8} \div \frac{1}{8} =$ _____

9. $\frac{300}{25} =$ _____

10. $35x \div 7xy =$ _____

11. $\frac{8ab}{b} =$ _____

12. $5 - {-3} =$ _____

13. $|0| =$ _____

14. $|{-21}| =$ _____

15. $15 - {-8} =$ _____

Name: _____ Date: _____

Chapter 5: Operations on Algebraic Expressions (cont.)

16. $20 \times -5 =$ _____

17. $100 \div -10 =$ _____

18. $-36 \div 6 =$ _____

19. $-3(6 + -2) =$ _____

20. $12 \div -6 + 4 - -7 =$ _____

21. $0 + y =$ _____

22. $0 - 13 =$ _____

23. $0 - (-12) =$ _____

24. $8xyz \bullet 0 =$ _____

25. $0 \div f =$ _____

26. $3 \div 0 =$ _____

27. $-7n \bullet 5y^2 =$ _____

28. $\dfrac{16b^2}{2b} =$ _____

29. $17t - 3t + 9t =$ _____

30. $21x + \dfrac{3}{4}x =$ _____

Chapter 5: Operations on Algebraic Expressions (cont.)

8 Algebraic Expressions Order of Operations

When solving mathematical expressions that have more than one operation, it is important to do the operations in the correct order.

1. Do the operations in the parentheses first.
2. Find the value of any number with an exponent.
3. Multiply and/or divide after the parentheses and exponents are done. If there are no parentheses, do the operations from left to right.
4. Add or subtract last. If there are no parentheses, do the operations from left to right.

Examples of Order of Operations:

1. Do the operations in the parentheses; if there are no parentheses, then do the operations from left to right.

Problem: $8(25 - 5) =$

Step 1: Do the operation in parentheses first: $(25 - 5) = 20$

So the problem is $8(20) =$

Step 2: Then multiply: $8(20) = 160$

Answer: $8(25 - 5) = 160$

Problem: $5 + (3 \times 5) =$

Step 1: Do the operation in parentheses first: $3 \times 5 = 15$.

Step 2: Then do the addition: $5 + 15 = 20$

Answer: $5 + (3 \times 5) = 20$

2. Find the value of any number with an exponent.

Problem: $5 \times 4^2 =$

Step 1: Find the value of the number with the exponent: $4^2 = 16$

Step 2: Then multiply: $5 \times 16 = 80$

Answer: $5 \times 4^2 = 80$

Chapter 5: Operations on Algebraic Expressions (cont.)

Problem: $16 \div 2^2 =$

Step 1: Find the value of the number with the exponent: $2^2 = 4$

Step 2: Then divide: $16 \div 4 = 4$

Answer: $16 \div 2^2 = 4$

3. Multiply or divide first, and then
4. Add or subtract.

Problem: $8 \times 5 + 4 \times 5 =$

Step 1: If there are no parentheses, go from left to right.

Step 2: Do the multiplication first: $8 \times 5 = 40$; $4 \times 5 = 20$

Step 3: Then do the addition: $40 + 20 = 60$

Answer: $8 \times 5 + 4 \times 5 = 60$

Problem: $25 \div 5 - 24 \div 6 =$

Step 1: If there are no parentheses, go from left to right.

Step 2: Divide first: $25 \div 5 = 5$; $24 \div 6 = 4$

Step 3: Subtract: $5 - 4 = 1$

Answer: $25 \div 5 - 24 \div 6 = 1$

Problem: $6 \times 5 - 4 \times 5 =$

Step 1: If there are no parentheses, go from left to right.

Step 2: Do the multiplication first: $6 \times 5 = 30$; $4 \times 5 = 20$

Step 3: Then subtract: $30 - 20 = 10$

Answer: $6 \times 5 - 4 \times 5 = 10$

Chapter 5: Operations on Algebraic Expressions (cont.)

9 Operating on Signed Numbers

The first part of this section has focused on the set of integers, {…, -3, -2, -1, 0, 1, 2, 3, …}, and how to add, subtract, multiply, and divide these types of numbers. There are other negative and positive numbers that are <u>not</u> integers.

Examples of Positive and Negative Numbers That Are Not Integers:

$$-\frac{1}{2} \qquad 0.76 \qquad -21.35 \qquad 4\frac{3}{4} \qquad -\sqrt{2}$$

Another way to ask the question is, how do I add, subtract, multiply, and divide real numbers, knowing that some are positive and some are negative? Every real number except 0 has a sign attached to it. We just use the results that work for integers.

Example:

$$\frac{\cancel{5}}{7} \times -\frac{3}{\cancel{10}} = \frac{1}{7} \times \frac{3}{-2} = -\frac{3}{14}$$

Solving this problem:

Step 1: A positive multiplied by a negative gives a negative answer.

Step 2: Multiply fractions as usual, simplifying any common factors.

Example:

$21.7 + -10.3 = 11.4$

Step 1: Since the addends differ in sign, find the difference.

$21.7 - 10.3 = 11.4$

Step 2: Take the answer as positive since |21.7| is bigger than |-10.3|.

In short, all earlier rules for signs still hold. Practice putting them into action with a variety of signed real numbers and the indicated operations.

$$14 \quad \frac{3}{786} \quad -52 \quad \frac{-7}{-7,209}$$

Name: _____   Date: _____

Chapter 5: Operations on Algebraic Expressions (cont.)

Practice: All Numbers, All Signs, Let's Operate!

Directions: Perform the necessary operations on the problems below.

1. $-\frac{3}{5} \times \frac{7}{8} =$ _____

2. $7.8 + -5.3 =$ _____

3. $-110 \div 2.5 =$ _____

4. $5\sqrt{3} + -11\sqrt{3} =$ _____

5. $-2.3 \times -10.2 =$ _____

6. $5 \times -36 =$ _____

7. $-\frac{2}{3} + \frac{5}{6}$ _____

8. $-\frac{10}{11} \div \frac{15}{22}$ _____

9. $2(4.7 + -3.6) =$ _____

10. $|-7 - -3.5| =$ _____

11. $8\sqrt{2} + -6\sqrt{2} =$ _____

12. $-3.71 - -4.2 =$ _____

13. $\frac{9}{10} - -\frac{2}{5} =$ _____

14. $-18.5 + 17.2 =$ _____

15. $-6.3 \times -10.3 =$ _____

Chapter 5: Operations on Algebraic Expressions (cont.)

Summary of Operations on Algebraic Expressions

Algebra uses numbers, symbols and letters. This section describes operations on numbers and algebraic expressions. Different symbols, shown in the table in the beginning of the worktext, mean different things. All symbols help describe the operations to be done in solving the problem. The letters represent or stand for some number that is unknown. This is called a variable. The number and variable operations in this section were addition, subtraction, multiplication, and division. When doing operations with numbers and variables that have more than one operation, it is important to do the operations in the correct order.

- We define the set of integers as $\{\ldots, -3, -2, -1, 0, 1, 2, 3, \ldots\}$

- Additive Inverse Property of Addition: Every real number, a, has a unique opposite, $-a$, so that $a + (-a) = 0$. The real number $-a$ is called the additive inverse of a.

- Adding Signed Numbers (integers or other real numbers):

    - Both Positive: Add as always and get a positive answer.

    - Both Negative: Add as if both positive and attach a negative sign to the answer.

    - Differing in Sign: Find the difference in the absolute values of the two numbers and attach the sign of the addend with the largest absolute value.

- Subtracting Signed Numbers: Using the Signed Number Subtraction Rule, change $a - b$ to $a + -b$.

- Multiplying Signed Numbers:

Sign of 1st factor	Sign of 2nd factor	Sign of product/answer
+	+	+
−	+	−
+	−	−
−	−	+

- Division of Signed Numbers: Think multiplication and use what you know!

Chapter 5: Operations on Algebraic Expressions (cont.)

Tips to Remember

1. Do the operations in the parentheses first.
2. Find the value of any number with an exponent.
3. Multiply and/or divide after the parentheses and exponents are done. If there are no parentheses, do the operations from left to right.
4. Add or subtract last. If there are no parentheses, do the operations from left to right.

It's all about using the inverse. Change subtraction to addition and division to multiplication!

$$-4 - 5 = ?$$ Think: $-4 + -5 = ?$
$$-20 \div 5 = ?$$ Think: $5 \times \text{what} = -20$

Real Life Applications of Operations on Algebraic Expressions

Number operations and order of operations are applied in bookkeeping, computers, and batting averages. Integers and signed numbers are used in describing temperatures, reporting golf scores (below par, even, over par), accounting, and in reporting the fluctuations in the stock market (up $1\frac{1}{2}$ or down -2).

Chapter 6: Equations and Problem Solving

Introduction to Equations and Problem Solving

One of the major goals of algebra is to solve problems. There are many strategies that can be used to solve problems. Some useful strategies include Making a Table and Guess, Check, and Revise to solve linear problems. Algebra uses equations to solve problems using variables. An equation uses numbers and variables to describe the relationship between two or more quantities. An equation is a mathematical statement that includes the use of an equal sign. Variables are letters used to identify an unknown number. There are many kinds of equations, but the most commonly used in algebra are linear and quadratic equations. This section covers strategies for problem solving, how to solve linear and quadratic equations, and using equations to solve problems.

Concepts of Equations and Problem Solving

1 Problem-Solving Strategies

    A Make a Table Strategy

    B Guess, Check, and Revise

    C Write an Equation

2 Solving Linear Equations

    A Equal Addition Rule

    B Equal Subtraction Rule

    C Equal Multiplication Rule

    D Equal Division Rule

    E Applications/Problem Solving

3 Solving Quadratic Equations

    A Factoring

    B Completing the Square

    C Quadratic Formula

    D Applications/Problem Solving

4 Polynomial Equations (Degree 3 and Higher)

    A Factoring

5 Rational Equations

    A Common Denominators

Should I make a Table or write an Equation?

63

Chapter 6: Equations and Problem Solving (cont.)

Explanations of Concepts of Equations and Problem Solving

1 **Problem-Solving Strategies**

When trying to solve a problem, it helps to have a systematic plan. One way of solving problems is using models. George Polya was a mathematician who devised a four-step plan for problem solving.

1. Understand the Problem
   - Identify what is known.
   - What are you asked to find?
   - Can you state the question in your own words?

2. Devise a Plan—Choose a Strategy
   - Would a table help organize the information?
   - Would a diagram or picture help?
   - Can I make a first estimate, test, and then revise to find the solution? (Guess, Check, and Revise)
   - Can I use a variable or write an equation that can be solved?

3. Carry Out the Plan—Put the Strategy to Work
   - Construct and fill in the table.
   - Draw the picture or diagram.
   - Make your best guess and follow through with tests and revision. (Guess, Check, and Revise)
   - Solve the equation.

4. Look Back
   - You have a solution.
   - Does it make sense? Is it reasonable?
   - Did you check your work?
   - Is there another approach that would give you the same answer?

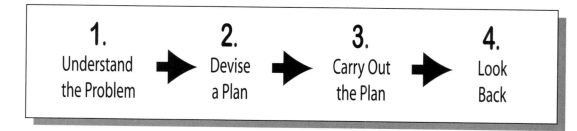

Chapter 6: Equations and Problem Solving (cont.)

Example of Problem Solving Using Polya's Process:

The costs for speeding tickets are determined in some states by fining the person a flat rate of $25 plus $20 for every mile per hour over the speed limit. The speed limit was 55. If a person was fined $225, how fast were they going?

SPEED LIMIT 55

1. Understand the Problem

   Identify what is known

   Flat rate is $25
   Fine is $20 per mph over the limit.
   Total fine was $225.
   Speed limit was 55.

   What do we want to know? How fast was the driver going?
   How many miles over the speed limit was the driver driving?

2. Devise a Plan, and
3. Carry Out the Plan

   For this problem, any one of three strategies could work. Each strategy will be shown showing that the final answer is the same in all three cases.

A **Make a Table Strategy**

# of Miles over the Limit	1	2	3	4	5	6	7	8	9	10
Cost of Fine	25 + 20(1) = 45	25 + 20(2)= 65	85	105	125	145	165	185	205	225

In filling out the table, the fine costs rise by $20 for each mph, so following the pattern, the fine of $225 is reached when the input of 10 miles over the speed limit is used.

Note that your table could have had entries by 2s or considered inputs by 5s—different choices would mean fewer or more trials to find the answer needed.

The solution of 10 mph over the limit checks out for a fine of $225. Have we answered the question?

Chapter 6: Equations and Problem Solving (cont.)

(B) **Guess, Check, and Revise**

Guess: The speed of the car was 75 mph.

That would mean that since $75 - 55 = 20$, the car was 20 mph over the limit.

Check: The fine would be $\$25 + \$20(20) = \$425$

Revise: $425 is too high, so you need to guess a car speed lower than 75.

Guess: The speed of the car was 65.

That would mean that since $65 - 55 = 10$, the car was traveling 10 mph over the limit.

Check: The fine would be $\$25 + \$20(10) = \$225$

That matches the given information! The car was traveling 10 mph over the speed limit of 55 mph.

The solution checks out. Have we answered the question?

(C) **Write an Equation**

Write the equation to describe the relationship between miles over the limit and the cost of the ticket.

Let x represent the number of miles over the 55 mph speed limit of the car.

Then, the flat rate plus $20 per mile over the limit should equal the total fine, $225.

Step 1: Translate that into an equation, $25 + 20x = 225$.

Step 2: Solve the equation.

- We want to find the value of x that makes the equation work. We want to isolate x by itself, or as we sometimes say, solve for x.
- Consider the equation—what is the first thing in the way of getting x by itself? The 25. How do we undo addition? Subtract! Just be sure to keep the balance by subtracting the same amount from each side of the equation.

$$\begin{array}{r} 25 + 20x = 225 \\ \underline{-25 \qquad\quad -25} \\ 20x = 200 \end{array}$$

Chapter 6: Equations and Problem Solving (cont.)

- What do you need to do next to find the the value of x? The only thing left is the 20 being multiplied to x. How do you undo multiplication? Divide! Just be sure to keep the balance of the equation by dividing both sides by the same amount.

$$20x = 200$$

$$\frac{20x}{20} = \frac{200}{20}$$

$$x = 10$$

Step 3: Check your work by using the answer. If you are 10 mph over the speed limit, your fine is $25 + $20(10) = $25 + $200 = $225

4. Look Back

Using each of the strategies, it was determined that the driver was 10 mph over the speed limit.

Have we answered the question asked in the original problem?

No, we need to know the speed of the car when ticketed. The driver went 10 miles over the 55 mph speed limit. The driver was going 10 + 55 = 65 miles per hour.

② Solving Linear Equations

A linear equation is any equation that can be put into the general form, $ax + b = 0$, where a and b can be any real numbers. Notice that the variable x is raised to the first power and that no other term can have a variable power higher than one. For example, $3x + d = 0$ and $-2t - 9 = 0$ are linear equations. Note that $-3x^2 + 5x + 1 = 0$ is not a linear equation because it contains a variable term raised to the second power.

The first assumption in solving equations is that there is a solution. When you solve an equation, you are trying to find a number to replace the variable to make the statement true. It may help to think of an equation as a balance. A balance is a level bar supported exactly in the middle. If there are equal weights on both ends of the balance and the weights are the same distance from the end of the balance, the balance remains level.

Chapter 6: Equations and Problem Solving (cont.)

If there is more weight on one end than the other, the balance no longer stays level.

Think of an equation as a balance where both sides must be the same to make the equation equal. As long as you do the same operation using the same number on each side of the equation, it does not change the solution of the equation.

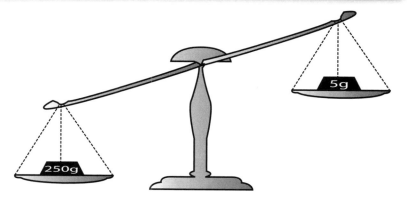

There are four rules for solving any type of equation.

A   **Equal Addition Rule**

If the same number is added to each side of an equation, the solutions of the original equation are the solutions of the new equation.

Add equal quantities to each side of the equation.

$x - 6 = 18$

Add the same quantity to each side $x - 6 + 6 = 18 + 6$

$x + (-6 + 6) = (18 + 6)$

$x + 0 = x$ and $18 + 6 = 24$

$x = 24$

Check the answer by substituting the number for x in the original equation.

$x - 6 = 18$

$24 - 6 = 18$

$18 = 18$, so the answer is correct.

B   **Equal Subtraction Rule**

If the same number is subtracted from each side of an equation, the solutions of the original equation are the solutions of the new equation.

Subtract equal quantities from each side of the equation:

$x + 2 = 11$

Subtract the same quantity from each side of the equation: $x + 2 - 2 = 11 - 2$

$x + (2 - 2 = 0) = (11 - 2 = 9)$

$x = 9$

Check the answer by substituting the number for x in the original equation.

$x + 2 = 11$

$9 + 2 = 11$

$11 = 11$, so the answer is correct.

Chapter 6: Equations and Problem Solving (cont.)

C   **Equal Multiplication Rule**

If each side of an equation is multiplied by the same number, the solutions of the original equations are the solutions of the new equation. Multiply each side by the same quantity.

$$\frac{1}{4}y = 5$$

The reciprocal of $\frac{1}{4}$ is 4, so multiply each side by 4.

$$\frac{1}{4}y \cdot 4 = 5 \cdot 4$$

$$y = 20$$

Check the answer by substituting the number for y in the original equation.

$$\frac{1}{4} \cdot 20 = 5$$

$$\frac{1}{4} \cdot \frac{20}{1}$$
$$\frac{20}{4} = 5$$

$5 = 5$, so the answer is correct.

D   **Equal Division Rule**

If each side of an equation is divided by the same number, the solutions of the original equation are the solutions of the new equation

Divide each side by the same quantity.
$$5a = 120$$

Divide each side by the same quantity: $\frac{5a}{5} = \frac{120}{5}$
$$a = 24$$

Check the answer by substituting the number for a in the original equation.

$$5a = 120$$
$$5 \times 24 = 120$$
So the answer is correct.

Chapter 6: Equations and Problem Solving (cont.)

E   **Problem-Solving Applications—Using Linear Equations to Solve Problems**

Examples of Using Linear Equations to Solve Problems:

Example Problem #1:

A gardener wants to fence in a rectangular flower bed using 42 feet of fencing. The length of the bed is to be twice the width. What are the dimensions of the flower bed?

Understand the Problem:

We know the perimeter for the rectangle—the distance around—has to be 42 feet. We know a relationship between the sides of the rectangle. We know how to find the perimeter, add 2 times the width to 2 times the length: $P = 2W + 2L$.

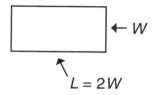

Devise a Plan: Write an equation using the information given.

Since $P = 2W + 2L$, we can make a few substitutions to form a linear equation to solve. We know that $P = 42$ feet, and we know that $L = 2W$.

Carry Out the Plan: This means that the equation we need to solve is:

$$42 = 2(W) + 2(2W)$$
$$42 = 2W + 4W$$
$$42 = 6W$$
$$\frac{42}{6} = \frac{6W}{6}$$
$$7 = W$$

Look Back:
We know the width is 7 feet. So, if the length is twice the width, the length will be 14 feet. Do these dimensions provide a perimeter of 42 feet? Let's check.

$$2(7) + 2(14) = 14 + 28 = 42$$

YES—it checks. Have we answered the question? YES—the dimensions of the garden will be 7 feet by 14 feet.

Chapter 6: Equations and Problem Solving (cont.)

Example Problem #2:

LaVon received 54 points on his last test. This represented a grade of 75% for the test. How many points were on the test?

Understand the Problem:
The problem can be restated as, 54 is 75% of what number?

Devise a Plan:
Write an equation—translate the sentence above into mathematical symbols, remembering that the word *is* translates to an equal sign and using x to represent the missing number. Also, remember to change 75% to its decimal equivalent 0.75 so we can compute.

Carry Out the Plan:
$54 = 0.75x$

$$\frac{54}{0.75} = \frac{0.75x}{0.75}$$

$72 = x$

Look Back:
Do we have a solution? YES, there were 72 points on the test.
Does this check? If we take 75% of 72, do we get 54? YES.

③ Solving Quadratic Equations

Quadratic equations are equations that include a term where the variable is raised to the second power (has an exponent of 2). In addition, no other term can include the variable raised to a higher power. The general form of a quadratic equation is $ax^2 + bx + c = 0$, where a, b, and c can be any real number.

Examples of Quadratic Equations:

$$2x^2 - 3x + 1 = 0 \qquad -5x^2 + 7 = 0 \qquad \tfrac{1}{2}x^2 + x = 0$$

Quadratic equations can also be formed when a linear equation is multiplied by the variable in the equation.

Chapter 6: Equations and Problem Solving (cont.)

Example of Forming a Quadratic Equation From Multiplying a Linear Equation By the Variable in the Equation:

$a(a + 8)$

$(a \bullet a) + (a \bullet 8)$

$a^2 + 8a$

$a(a + 8) = a^2 + 8a$

Quadratic equations can also be formed when two binomial expressions are multiplied together. There are five steps to multiply two binomial expressions.

Step 1: Multiply the two first terms.

Step 2: Multiply the two outside terms.

Step 3: Multiply the two inside terms.

Step 4: Multiply the two last terms.

Step 5: Add the terms together.

Example of Forming a Quadratic Equation From Multiplying Two Binomial Expressions:

Problem: $(y - 5)(y - 3)$

Step 1: Multiply the two first terms. $y \bullet y = y^2$

Step 2: Multiply the two outside terms. $y \bullet -3 = -3y$

Step 3: Multiply the two inside terms. $-5 \bullet y = -5y$

Step 4: Multiply the two last terms. $-5 \bullet -3 = 15$

Step 5: Add the terms together. $y^2 + -3y + -5y + 15 = y^2 + -8y + 15$

Answer: $(y - 5)(y - 3) = y^2 - 8y + 15$

When multiplying binomial expressions, multiply the **F**irst terms, **O**utside terms, **I**nside terms, and then the **L**ast terms. **FOIL** is an easy way to remember the necessary steps to complete the multiplication.

Quadratic equations can be solved by using one or more of these methods: factoring, completing the square, or using the quadratic formula.

Chapter 6: Equations and Problem Solving (cont.)

(A) **Solving Quadratic Equations by Factoring**

The easiest way of solving quadratic equations is by factoring. To factor quadratic equations, they must first be put into standard form and then simplified. The standard form of a quadratic equation is $ax^2 + bx + c = 0$ where $a \neq 0$.

Example of Putting an Equation in Standard Form:

$3x^2 - 7x = 4$
Put into standard form by adding or subtracting the same terms from both sides of the equation: $3x^2 - 7x - 4 = 4 - 4$
Simplify: $3x^2 - 7x - 4 = 0$

Now that the equation is in standard form, the quadratic equation can be solved by factoring. There are three types of quadratic equations in standard form. Type I has only two terms and has the form of $ax^2 + c = 0$. Type I does not include an x term. Type II has only two terms and has the form $ax^2 + bx = 0$. Type II does not include a constant term—the number term. Type III quadratic equations have all three terms and have the form $ax^2 + bx + c = 0$ where $a \neq 0$. How to use factoring to solve each of these three types of standard form quadratic equations will be shown in the following examples.

Example of Solving Type I Quadratic Equations in Standard Form by Factoring:

Problem: $a^2 - 49 = 0$

Step 1: Add or subtract to move the a^2 term to one side of the equation.

$a^2 - 49 + 49 = 49 + 0$

$a^2 - 0 = 49$

Step 2: Multiply or divide to eliminate the coefficient in front of the a; in this case the coefficient is one, so $1 \cdot a^2 = a^2$.

$a^2 = 49$

Step 3: Take the square root of both sides of the equal signs.

$\sqrt{a^2} = \pm\sqrt{49}$

Answer: $a = \pm 7$

Step 4: Check your answer by replacing the a with 7 or -7.

$7^2 - 49 = 0$	$-7^2 - 49 = 0$
$7^2 = 7 \times 7 = 49$	$-7^2 = -7 \times -7 = 49$
$49 - 49 = 0$	$49 - 49 = 0$

Chapter 6: Equations and Problem Solving (cont.)

Example of Solving Type II Quadratic Equations in Standard Form by Factoring:

Problem: $x^2 + 10x = 0$

Step 1: Factor an x out of the equation.

$x(x + 10) = 0$

Step 2: Set both factors equal to zero.

$x = 0$ $x + 10 = 0$

Step 3: Solve both equations.

Answers: $x = 0$ $x + 10 = 0$

$x + 10 - 10 = 0 - 10$

$x + 0 = \text{-}10$

$x = \text{-}10$

Step 4: Check your answer by substituting the value of x in the original equation.

$x^2 + 10x = 0$

$(\text{-}10)^2 + 10(\text{-}10) = 0$

Simplify.

$100 + \text{-}100 = 0$

Example of Solving Type III Quadratic Equations in Standard Form by Factoring:

Step 1: Put equation in standard form.

Problem: $x^2 - 5x + 4 = 0$

Step 2: Factor the x^2 term.

$x^2 = (x)(x)$

$(x \quad)(x \quad) = 0$

Step 3: List pairs of factors in numerical terms.

Numerical term is 4, so factors could be:

$(2)(2) = 4$

$(\text{-}2)(\text{-}2) = 4$

$(\text{-}1)(\text{-}4) = 4$

$(1)(\text{-}4) = \text{-}4$

Chapter 6: Equations and Problem Solving (cont.)

Step 4: Place one pair of factors in the parentheses. Check to see if multiplying the two binomial expressions results in the original equation. (Note: use FOIL.) If not, try another pair of factors until the correct pair is found.

$(x + 2)(x + 2) = 0$

First terms

$(x)(x) = x^2$

Outside terms

$(x)(2)$

Inside terms

$(2)(x)$

$x^2 + 2x + 2x + 4$

$x^2 + 4x + 4$

Not the original equation, try another pair.

$(x - 4)(x - 1) = 0$

First terms

$(x)(x) = x^2$

Outside terms

$(x)(-1)$

Inside terms

$(-4)(x)$

Add them all together.

$x^2 + (-4x) + (-1x) + (4)(1)$

Simplify.

$x^2 - 5x + 4 = 0$

This is the original equation.

$x^2 - 5x + 4 = 0$

 FIRST TERMS

 OUTSIDE TERMS

 INSIDE TERMS

 LAST TERMS

Step 5: Set each binomial expression equal to zero.

$x - 4 = 0 \qquad x - 1 = 0$

Chapter 6: Equations and Problem Solving (cont.)

Step 6: Solve each equation.

$x - 4 = 0$

$x - 4 + 4 = 0 + 4$

Answers: $x = 4$

$x - 1 = 0$

$x - 1 + 1 = 0 + 1$

$x = 1$

Step 7: Check the answers.

Substitute 4 into the original equation.

$4^2 - 5(4) + 4 = 0$

$16 - 20 + 4 = 0$

$0 = 0$, so 4 is correct.

Now substitute the 1 in the equation.

$x^2 - 5x + 4 = 0$

$1^2 - (5)(1) + 4$

$1 - 5 + 4 = 0$

$-4 + 4 = 0$

$0 = 0$, so 1 is correct.

B   **Solving Quadratic Equations by Completing the Square**

When a quadratic equation does not resolve into a factored form, it can be resolved by completing the square. Completing the square method works by finding a constant quantity (a number) that is added to both sides of the equation to make it look like a perfect square.

Example of Completing the Square Method to Solve a Quadratic Equation:

Problem: $x^2 + 2x = 1$

Step 1: Make it look like a perfect square by adding 1 to both sides.

$x^2 + 2x + 1 = 1 + 1$

$x^2 + 2x + 1 = 2$

Step 2: The equation can now be factored.

$(x + 1)^2 = 2$

Step 3: The solution can be found by taking the square root of each side.

$\sqrt{(x + 1)^2} = \pm\sqrt{2}$

Chapter 6: Equations and Problem Solving (cont.)

So,

$x + 1 = \pm\sqrt{2}$

$x + 1 - 1 = \pm\sqrt{2} - 1$

$x = \pm\sqrt{2} - 1$

Answers: $x = \sqrt{2} - 1$ or $x = -\sqrt{2} - 1$ are the two solutions for the equation.

Ⓒ   Solving Quadratic Equations Using the Quadratic Formula

Quadratic equations can also be solved using the Quadratic Formula. First put the formula in standard form $ax^2 + bx + c = 0$. Figure out the values of a, b, and c. Substitute the values for a, b, and c into the equation below and solve it. Then check your answer. Using the quadratic formula, you may get zero, one, or two answers.

Quadratic Formula

For any equation of the form $ax^2 + bx + c = 0$, the solutions to the equation are given by:

$$x = \frac{-b \pm \sqrt{b^2 - 4ac}}{2a}$$

Example of Solving a Quadratic Equation with the Quadratic Formula:

Problem: $x^2 + 2x + 1 = 0$

Step 1: Put the quadratic equation in standard form. $ax^2 + bx + c = 0$. This equation is in standard form.

$x^2 + 2x + 1 = 0$

Step 2: Find the values of a, b, and c.

x^2 has the coefficient of 1, so $a = 1$.

$2x$ has the coefficient of 2, so $b = 2$.

The number in the equation is 1, so $c = 1$.

Step 3: Substitute a, b, and c into the quadratic formula.

Quadratic Formula

$$x = \frac{-b \pm \sqrt{b^2 - 4ac}}{2a} = \frac{-2 \pm \sqrt{2^2 - 4(1)(1)}}{2(1)}$$

77

Chapter 6: Equations and Problem Solving (cont.)

Step 4: Compute the values under the radical sign first

$$\frac{-2 \pm \sqrt{2^2 - 4(1)(1)}}{2(1)} \Rightarrow \frac{-2 \pm \sqrt{4 - 4}}{2(1)} \Rightarrow \frac{-2 \pm \sqrt{0}}{2(1)} \Rightarrow \frac{-2 \pm 0}{2(1)} \Rightarrow \frac{-2 \pm 0}{2(1)} \Rightarrow \frac{-2}{2} = -1$$

Step 5: Check the answer.

Substitute -1 in the original equation.

$x^2 + 2x + 1$
$= (-1)^2 + 2(-1) + 1$
$= 1 + (-2) + 1$
$= -1 + 1$
$= 0$

Answer: So $x = -1$ is the correct answer.
$x^2 + 2x + 1 = 0$ when $x = -1$

D   **Quadratic Equation Applications/Problem Solving**

Quadratic equations can be used to solve everyday problems. If you were trying to carpet a rectangular room, you could use a quadratic equation to solve the problem. The width of a rectangular room is 10 meters less than the length of the room. The surface area of the floor in the room is 600 square meters. What are the length and the width of the floor in the room?

Step 1: What is known?
The width of the room is 10 meters less than the length.
Use l to represent the length so the width is $(l - 10)$.

Step 2: To find the surface area, multiply the length times the width.
So $l(l - 10)$ is the area of the floor.
The area of the floor is 600 square meters.
So $l(l - 10) = 600$ square meters.

Step 3: Multiply the equation.
$l^2 - 10l = 600$ square meters

Step 4: Put equation in standard form. $ax^2 + bx + c = 0$
$l^2 - 10l - 600 = 600 - 600$
$l^2 - 10l - 600 = 0$

Chapter 6: Equations and Problem Solving (cont.)

Step 5: Factor the equation.

$(l-30)(l+20) = 0$

Step 6: Solve for l.

If $l-30 = 0$, then $l = 30$.

If $l+20 = 0$, then $l = -20$.

Step 7: The length of the floor cannot be a negative number, so the length must be 30 meters.

The width is $l-10$, so $30-10 = 20$. The width = 20 meters.
Surface area is length times the width, and the surface area of the room is 600 square meters.
(30 meters)(20 meters) = 600 square meters, so the answer is correct.

4　Polynomial Equations (Degree 3 and Higher)

Polynomial equations are named by the term of highest degree. The degree of a polynomial is the greatest of the degrees of its terms after it has been simplified. The equations in the previous section were linear and quadratic. A linear equation has the general form $ax + b = 0$ and is a degree one polynomial equation. A quadratic equation is represented by the general form $ax^2 + bx + c = 0$ and is called a degree two polynomial equation. Cubic equations are represented by $ax^3 + bx^2 + cx + d = 0$. It is a degree three polynomial equation. This section will introduce polynomial equations that are degree three and higher.

A　Factoring

To solve these polynomial equations, put the equation into standard form. Factor the left side. Set each factor equal to zero and solve. Check the solutions in the original equation. Polynomial equations can also be factored by using the greatest common factor (GCF). The GCF for a polynomial is the largest monomial that divides or is a factor of each term of the polynomial. When factoring polynomials higher than degree 3, you may factor by grouping.

Example of Solving Polynomial Equations Degree 3 by Factoring:

Problem: $18x^3 + 8x + 24x^2 = 0$

Step 1: Put into standard form, $ax^3 + bx^2 + cx + d = 0$.

$18x^3 + 24x^2 + 8x = 0$

Step 2: Factor completely.

$2x(9x^2 + 12x + 4) = 0$

$2x(3x + 2)^2 = 0$

Chapter 6: Equations and Problem Solving (cont.)

Step 3: Solve by inspection or set each factor = 0.

$$2x = 0 \qquad (3x + 2)^2$$
$$x = 0 \quad \text{or} \quad x = -\tfrac{2}{3} \quad \text{or} \quad x = -\tfrac{2}{3}$$

Step 4: Check your answers in the original equation.

$$18x^3 + 8x + 24x^2 \qquad\qquad 18x^3 + 8x + 24x^2$$

$$= 18(0)^3 + 8(0) + 24(0)^2 \qquad 18(-\tfrac{2}{3})^3 + 8(-\tfrac{2}{3}) + 24(-\tfrac{2}{3})^2$$

$$= 0 + 0 + 0 \qquad\qquad 18(-\tfrac{8}{27}) + 8(-\tfrac{2}{3}) + 24(-\tfrac{4}{9})$$

$$= 0$$

Answers: $x = 0$ is a solution $-\tfrac{144}{27} + -\tfrac{144}{27} + \tfrac{288}{27}$

$$-\tfrac{288}{27} + \tfrac{288}{27} = 0$$

$$x = -\tfrac{2}{3} \text{ is a solution}$$

Example of Solving Polynomial Equations Higher than Degree 3 by Using Grouping:

Problem: $x^2 + 5bx - 2ax - 10ab$

Step 1: Put into standard form. $x^2 + 5bx - 2ax - 10ab = 0$

Step 2: Find the greatest common factor. There is no greatest common factor.

Step 3: Factor by grouping.

$$x^2 + 5bx - 2ax - 10ab$$

$x(x + 5b) - 2a(x + 5b) =$ Factor out the GCF from each group.

$$\frac{x(x + 5b)}{x + 5b} - \frac{2a(x + 5b)}{x + 5b} \qquad \text{Factor out the GCF of } (x + 5b).$$

$$(x + 5b)(x - 2a)$$

Step 4: Solve by inspection, or set each factor = 0.

$$(x + 5b)(x - 2a)$$

$$
\begin{array}{ll}
x + 5b = 0 & x - 2a = 0 \\
x + 5b - 5b = 0 - 5b & x - 2a + 2a = 0 + 2a \\
\end{array}
$$

Answers: $x = -5b \qquad\qquad x = 2a$

Chapter 6: Equations and Problem Solving (cont.)

Step 5: Check your answer.

$x^2 + 5bx - 2ax - 10ab = 0$ $x^2 + 5bx - 2ax - 10ab = 0$

$(-5b)^2 + 5b(-5b) - 2a(-5b) - 10ab$ $(2a)^2 + 5b(2a) - 2a(2a) - 10ab = 0$

$25b^2 - 25b^2 + 10ab - 10ab = 0$ $4a^2 + 10ab - 4a^2 - 10ab = 0$

The solutions are correct.

5 Rational Equations

A rational number is a real number that can be expressed as the quotient of two integers. The steps to solving rational equations are to remove the fractions by multiplying by the lowest common denominator to solve the remaining equation. Check for extraneous solutions. Extraneous solutions for rational equations are values that cause any denominator to be 0. If 0 is in the denominator, then the expression is undefined. So all values that cause the denominator to be zero would be discarded.

A Common Denominators

Example of Solving Rational Equations by Converting to Common Denominator:

Problem: $\dfrac{x-1}{25} = \dfrac{2}{5}$

Step 1: Multiply by the lowest common denominator.

$$\left(\frac{25}{1}\right)\frac{x-1}{25} = \frac{2}{5}\left(\frac{25}{1}\right)$$

$$\left(\frac{\overset{1}{\cancel{25}}}{1}\right)\frac{x-1}{\underset{1}{\cancel{25}}} = \frac{2}{\underset{1}{\cancel{5}}}\left(\frac{\overset{5}{\cancel{25}}}{1}\right)$$

$$x - 1 = 10$$

Step 2: Solve the remaining equation.

$x - 1 = 10$

$x - 1 + 1 = 10 + 1$

Answer: $x = 11$

Chapter 6: Equations and Problem Solving (cont.)

Step 3: Check for extraneous solutions.

11 does not cause any denominator to be zero, so it is not an extraneous solution.

Example of Solving Rational Equations:

Problem: $\dfrac{7}{a} - \dfrac{1}{3} = \dfrac{5}{a}$

Step 1: Remove the fractions by multiplying by the lowest common denominator.

$$(3a)\left(\dfrac{7}{a} - \dfrac{1}{3}\right) = \dfrac{5}{a}(3a)$$

$$\dfrac{3a}{1}\left(\dfrac{7}{a}\right) - \dfrac{3a}{1}\left(\dfrac{1}{3}\right) = \dfrac{5}{a}\left(\dfrac{3a}{1}\right)$$

$$\dfrac{21a}{a} - \dfrac{3a}{3} = \dfrac{15a}{a}$$

$$21 - a = 15$$

Step 2: Solve the remaining equation.

$$21 - a = 15$$
$$21 - a - 21 = 15 - 21$$
$$-a = -6$$
$$\dfrac{-a}{-1} = \dfrac{-6}{-1}$$

Answer: $a = 6$

Step 3: Check for extraneous solutions.

6 does not cause any denominator to be zero, so it is not an extraneous solution.

Name: _____ Date: _____

Chapter 6: Equations and Problem Solving (cont.)

Practice: Equations and Problem Solving

Directions: Solve the following algebraic equations. Show your work.

Form a quadratic equation from a linear equation by multiplying by the variable in the equation.

1. $x(5x + 8) = 0$ _____

2. $-a(10a - 2) = 0$ _____

3. $4x(2x - 3) = -3$ _____

Form quadratic equations from multiplying binomial expressions.

4. $(2c - 5)(3c + 1) = 0$ _____

5. $(x + 2)(x - 3) = 0$ _____

Use factoring to solve questions 6–8.

6. $3x^2 - 27 = 0$ _____

7. $2a^2 - 6a = 0$ _____

8. $2b^2 + 7b = -6$ _____

Use the "Complete the Square Method" to solve question 9.

9. $x^2 + 6x + 7 = 0$ _____

Name: _____ Date: _____

Chapter 6: Equations and Problem Solving (cont.)

Use the Quadratic Formula to solve questions 10 and 11.

10. $2x^2 + 5x + 2 = 0$ _____ **11.** $3x^2 + x - 2 = 0$ _____

Solve using a quadratic equation.

12. Ian wanted to build a dog pen for his new beagle. He used the wall of the house for one side. He bought 20 meters of fence to build the other 3 sides. Find the dimensions of the pen if the area is 48 square meters.

_____

Solve polynomial equations of degree 3 by factoring.

13. $18x^3 + 66x^2 - 24x = 0$ _____

Solve polynomial equations higher than degree 3 by factoring.

14. $ax - ay - bx + by$ _____

Solve rational equations with common denominators.

15. $\dfrac{b-2}{15} = \dfrac{2}{5}$ _____ **16.** $\dfrac{3}{x+2} - \dfrac{1}{x} = \dfrac{1}{5x}$ _____

Chapter 6: Equations and Problem Solving (cont.)

Summary of Equations and Problem Solving

Problems can be solved in a variety of ways. This section introduced you to Polya's four stages of problem solving:

- Understand the Problem
- Devise a Plan—Choose a Strategy!
- Carry Out the Plan—Put the Strategy to Work
- Look Back

Solving Equations

- Simplify each side of the equation using the rules for the orders of operations.
- What do you need to do to find out what the variable is? There are two possible steps:
  1. Add and/or subtract the same number and/or variable from both sides of the equation.
  2. Multiply and/or divide both sides of the equation by the same number.
- Always Look Back! Check your work using the answer.

Linear equations are simple equations with numbers and/or variables. An example of a linear equation is $ax + b = 0$.

Equal Addition Rule

If the same number is added to each side of an equation, then the roots of the original equation are the roots of the new equation.

Equal Subtraction Rule

If the same number is subtracted from each side of an equation, then the roots of the original equation are the roots of the new equation.

Equal Multiplication Rule

If each side of an equation is multiplied by the same number, then the roots of the original equation are the roots of the new equation.

Equal Division Rule

If each side of an equation is divided by the same number, then the roots of the original equation are the roots of the new equation.

Polynomial equations are named by the term of highest degree. The degree of a polynomial is the greatest of the degrees of its terms after it has been simplified. Quadratic equations are polynomial equations of degree two. An example is $2x^2 + 4x - 5 = 0$. Quadratic equations can be simplified by using one or more of the following methods: factoring, completing the square, or using the quadratic formula.

Chapter 6: Equations and Problem Solving (cont.)

To solve polynomial equations of three degrees or higher, put the equation into standard form. Factor the left side. Set each factor equal to zero and solve. Check the solutions in the original equation. Polynomial equations can also be factored by using the greatest common factor (GCF). The GCF for a polynomial is the largest monomial that divides or is a factor of each term of the polynomial. When factoring polynomials higher than degree 3, you may factor by grouping.

A rational number is a real number that can be expressed as the quotient of two integers. The steps to solving rational equations are to remove the fractions by multiplying by the lowest common denominator to solve the remaining equation. Check for extraneous solutions.

Tips to Remember

When multiplying binomial expressions, multiply the **F**irst terms, **O**utside terms, **I**nside terms, and then the **L**ast terms. "FOIL" is an easy way to remember the necessary steps to complete the multiplication.

Scientists have discovered that using THE scientific method to solve problems leads to misconceptions that there is only one way to solve problems. The authors do not want to leave you with the misconception that there is only one "right" way to solve problems. The Polya Process, looking for patterns, using models and diagrams, making tables, and using equations are only a few strategies for solving problems. There are many ways to solve problems. Students may use different methods to get the same answers. Students need to use what makes sense to them when solving problems.

Real Life Applications of Equations and Problem Solving

Linear equations can be used in studying the speed of different wildlife, population studies, page layout and design, temperature change, marine biology, framing pictures, and finding costs, rates, averages, and percentages. Linear equations are also used in ecology, chemistry, retail sales, and purchasing.

Chapter 7: Graphing

Introduction to Graphing

In solving many types of problems, graphing becomes a useful approach. Being able to look at information in a visual form provides another way to find answers and to uncover patterns. In this section, the basics of how to use a coordinate plane to show number relationships will be covered. In many cases, the problems of algebra involve the relationship between two quantities. For example: Are height and shoe size related? If you know that I am 5 feet 5 inches tall, can you predict what size shoe I wear? If you know how many people are attending a football game, can you predict the number of soft drinks that will be sold? Being able to look at ordered pairs of numbers by plotting them on a grid with directional axes can help determine answers and predict solutions to algebraic problems.

Concepts of Graphing

1   Cartesian Coordinate System or Coordinate Plane

         x-axis and *y*-axis

         Quadrants

         Origin

         Ordered Pairs

         Plotting Ordered Pairs

Explanations of Concepts of Graphing

1   **Cartesian Coordinate System or Coordinate Plane**

The use of a grid to represent locations in the plane becomes a useful tool in algebra and problem solving. A **plane** is a two-dimensional surface—much like a piece of paper that continues to extend infinitely in all directions. The notion of using a grid or a coordinate system to represent information was first envisioned and used by the mathematician René Descartes. For this reason, it is sometimes referred to as the **Cartesian coordinate system**. In the figure on the next page, a typical representation of this grid system or coordinate plane is shown. Notice that it works by putting two number lines together. The number line that measures distance from left to right (horizontally), moving from negative number values to positive number values, is called the **x-axis**. This *x*-axis is essentially the number line discussed and used in representing the real number system in earlier sections of this work text. The number line that measures distance from bottom to top (vertically), moving from negative values to positive values, is called the **y-axis**.

By breaking up the plane using these two axes, the plane is divided into four sections or quarters, called **quadrants**. The four quadrants are typically labeled using Roman numerals (I, II, III, and IV) and are numbered moving in a counterclockwise direction from the upper right.

Chapter 7: Graphing (cont.)

Example of the Cartesian Coordinate System:

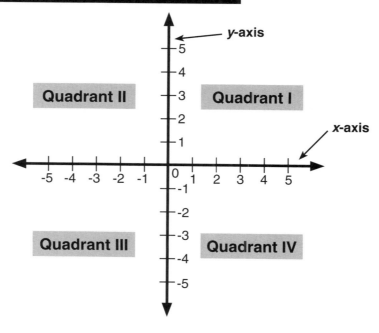

To mark a location on the coordinate plane with a dot means to **plot a point** and requires that two numbers be used. The two numbers form what is known as an **ordered pair**. An ordered pair is shown by using parentheses to enclose the pair of numbers with the numbers separated by a comma. For example, (-2, 5) is an ordered pair. The first number in the pair, -2, indicates how far right or left to move along the *x*-axis. Since it is a negative 2, we move left two units. The second number in the pair, 5, indicates how far up or down to move along the *y*-axis. Since it is positive 5, we move up 5 units and place a point in that location. Always start from the intersection point for the two number lines. The point that marks the intersection of the *x*- and *y*-axes is called the **origin** and is denoted with the ordered pair (0, 0).

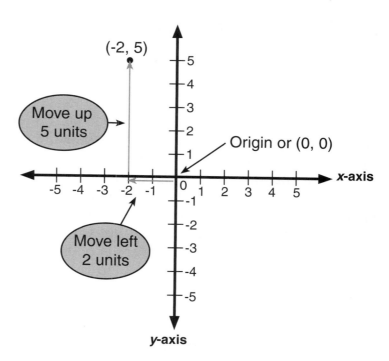

Name: _____   Date: _____

Chapter 7: Graphing (cont.)

Practice: Orderly Ordered Pairs Graphing

1. In what quadrant would the point (-3, 5) be located? _____

2. Give an example of a point that would be found in Quadrant IV. _____

3. Plot the following set of points on the provided coordinate plane. If you connect the dots in each group, in the order listed, you should notice something. What is it?
    Group 1: (-8, -3), (-8, 4), (-6, 0), (-4, 5), (-4, -2)
    Group 2: (-2.5, -2.5), (-1.5, 0), (0, 3), (1.5, 5), (3, -4)
    Group 3: (2, 5), (7, 5)
    Group 4: (4, 5), (4, -1)
    Group 5: (6, 2.5), (6, -9)
    Group 6: (6, -4), (9, -4)
    Group 7: (9, 4), (9, -9)

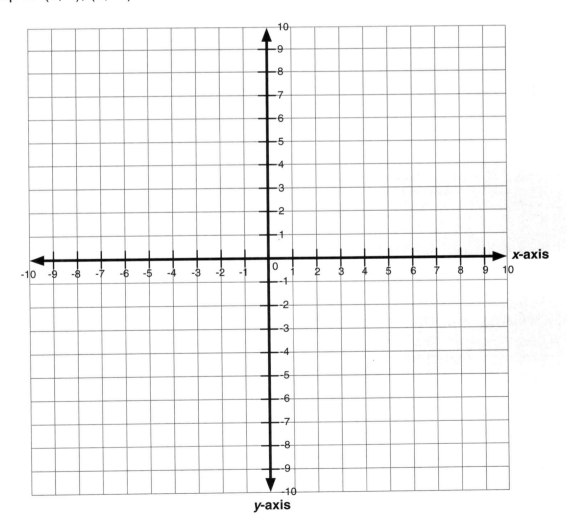

Chapter 7: Graphing (cont.)

Summary of Graphing

Graphing can be used as a visual representation of the relationship between two different things—like arm span versus height.

Tips to Remember

Think of the *x*- and *y*-axes as two perpendicular real number lines that continue to infinity, laid out on a grid. The place where they intersect is the point (0, 0), or the origin.

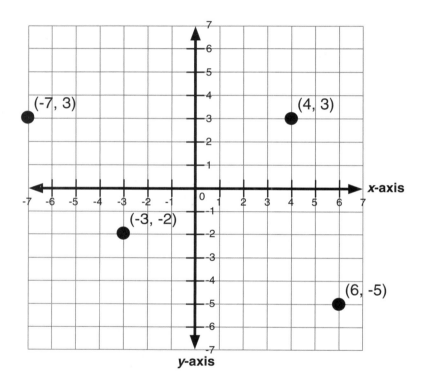

Real Life Applications of Graphing

Graphs are used to determine trends in shopping patterns, scores, and data collected in an investigation. Graphs are also used to make predictions. When determining whether or not an object can sink or float in water, a graph can be used. Density is the mass per unit volume. If data on the mass and volume of each object is collected for a set of objects, the mass and volume become plot points on the graph. When these plot points can be plotted and compared to the density of water, you can determine whether the object will sink or float.

90

Chapter 8: Functions

Introduction to Functions

A function can be defined most simply as a mathematical rule. A function provides the information necessary to pair an input number with an output number. One way to envision what a function does is to think of it as a machine. You drop a number into the machine, and after some work, the function machine provides you with an output number generated by the machine's rule. Understanding what a function is and how to use the mathematical notation is the focus of this section. Functions allow us to construct rules that tell us how bank accounts generate interest over time, how long it takes for radioactive materials to decay, and how to change a Celsius temperature into a Fahrenheit temperature.

Concepts of Functions

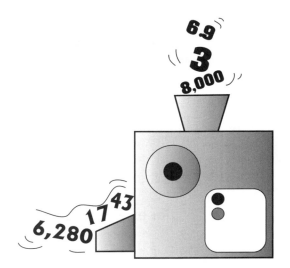

1 Definition of a Function

      Domain

      Range

2 Representations of Functions

    A Tables

    B Graphs

    C Function Notation, $f(x)$

Explanations of Concepts of Functions

1 Definition of a Function

A **function** is a rule that pairs a number from one set with a number in a second set. It provides a description of a relationship between two variables—an input variable and an output variable. In a function, the output variable depends on the input variable. This means that the input variable is the independent variable, and the output variable is the dependent variable.

There is another important restriction in calling a rule a function. A rule is only defined as a function if it sends every element of the first set (the **domain**) to exactly one element in the second set (the **range**).

Definition: A variable y is a function of a variable x if each value of x is assigned to exactly one value of y. The set of input values is called the domain, and the set of output values is called the range.

Chapter 8: Functions (cont.)

Let's look at some examples to illustrate rules that are functions, and rules that are not functions.

Example of a Function:

If you have this set of plot points or ordered pairs, is it a function?

{(1, 2), (3, 4), (5, 6)}

Does each input (domain), or the first number in the pair, have only one corresponding output (range) to the second number in the pair?

The domain values are {1, 3, 5}.

Range values are {2, 4, 6}.

Yes, the domain values only have one range value, so it is a function.

Example of a Function:

The figure below shows a relationship between two sets that fits the definition of a function.

Pick any domain element and trace where it is sent.

Is it sent to one and only one element in the range set? Yes.

For example, -2 is sent to 0 and only 0.

Is it all right that -5 is also sent to 0? Yes, because 5 is sent to 0 and only zero. So, lots of things from the domain can be sent to the same output element—that still fits the definition of function.

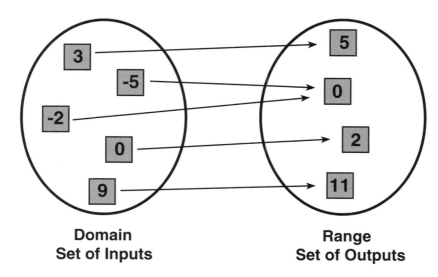

Domain
Set of Inputs

Range
Set of Outputs

Chapter 8: Functions (cont.)

Example That Is Not A Function:

If you have this set of plot points, or ordered pairs, is it a function?
{(1, 2), (1, 4), (5, 6)}

Does each input (domain), or first number, have only one corresponding output (range), or second number, in the pair?

The domain values are {1, 1, 5}.
Range values are {2, 4, 6}.

No, this is not a function. The domain values do not only have one range value. Two of the ordered pairs have a domain of 1 with a different range value, so it is not a function.

Example That Is Not A Function:

The figure below shows a relationship between two sets that does not fit the definition of a function.

It is a rule between two sets but fails to be a function. Why?

Pick the domain element 9 and trace where the rule sends it. The illustration shows it being sent to 2 and to 11. Is that OK for a function? No, each input should be sent to one and only one output!

So even though the input 3 is sent only to 5, the function definition fails for at least one of the input elements, and because of this is not the rule of a function.

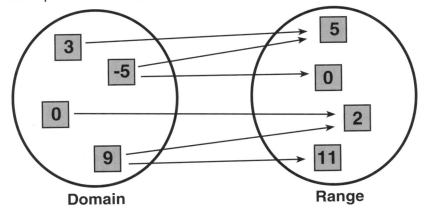

Domain   **Range**

In working with functions, we typically use *x* to represent the independent variable (**input**) and *y* to represent the dependent variable (**output**). While we could use pictures as in the previous examples, there are other ways to represent a function, the relationship between two variables.

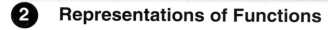

Chapter 8: Functions (cont.)

2 **Representations of Functions**

A **Tables**

One way to show the relationship between the two variables, to indicate the rule or function that pairs them, is to use a table. Sometimes these tables are called *x-y* tables and sometimes T-tables. The table consists of two columns. The first is the *x* column, or input column, and the second is the *y* column, or the output column. By looking at the table, the function can be defined. Let's look at some tables and see if they actually define functions.

Example:

x	y
-1	0
5	6
0	1
7	8

This table defines a function. Why? Each input value in the *x*-column is paired with exactly one output value in the *y*-column. The use of the table is easier and more efficient than drawing a picture with circles and arrows. Can you describe in words what the function rule is for this example? To find the output, add one to the input.

Example:

x	y
-1	1
5	0
0	-5
7	8
7	6

This table does not define a function. Why? There is at least one input value that has more than one output value. The table indicates that 7 has the output values of 8 and 6. That contradicts the definition of a function where each input value has only one output value.

Chapter 8: Functions (cont.)

B  Graphs

Another way to show the relationship between two variables, the rule connecting domain values to range values, is to plot the ordered pairs generated on a coordinate plane. For example, we can take the table values from a function rule and think of them as ordered pairs, (*x, y*). These ordered pairs can then be plotted on a coordinate plane to provide a graph of the function.

Example:

x	y
-1	0
5	6
0	1
7	8

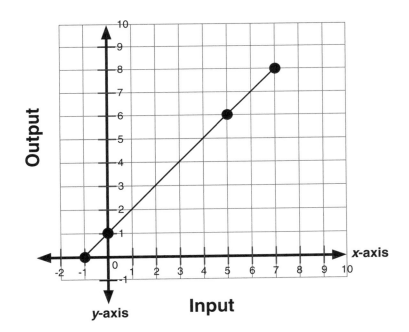

Chapter 8: Functions (cont.)

 C **Function Notation, $f(x)$**

In dealing with function rules, the representation used most often is the use of function notation. This is a representation that allows us to take advantage of what we understand about equations in this new situation involving two variables. As noted earlier in this section, we will use the variable x to represent the domain values and the variable y to represent the range values. We can then write the rule as an equation in x and y. For example, an earlier function was described as "taking the input and adding one to it to get the output." If we think about using variables and what we know about equations, this rule can be represented as, $y = x + 1$. Translated, the equation says, "you find the output y by taking x and adding one" or "y is $x + 1$."

Sometimes we use a more formal notation to indicate the function and the output. Instead of using y, we use $f(x)$. Literally, the notation $f(x)$, indicates the function, f, and the fact that f acts on x, the input. We read $f(x)$, as "f of x," meaning the result of f on the input x yields the output. In a sense, think of y and $f(x)$ as interchangeable. While $f(x)$ is the typical notation used, other lowercase letters can represent functions, just as other variables can be used in place of x to represent the domain or input values. For example, $g(t) = 5 \cdot t + 4$ is another example of the use of function notation. The letter in the parentheses is the input or independent variable.

Example:

Suppose a function is defined in function notation as follows:

$$f(x) = 2x^2 + x + 1$$

What output goes with an input of 3? If $x = 3$, what is $f(3)$?

To find the output value, substitute 3 for x in the rule:

$$f(x) = 2(3)^2 + 3 + 1 = 2 \cdot 9 + 3 + 1 = 18 + 3 + 1 = 22$$

So, (3, 22) is an ordered pair that satisfies the rule given for $f(x)$.

Function rules can use any of the operations, exponents, radicals, and real numbers that have been reviewed in earlier sections of this worktext. The following sections in this worktext and the Algebra II worktext will deal with specific types of functions—linear, quadratic, rational, and exponential—and how to work with those types of function equations.

Name: _____ Date: _____

Chapter 8: Functions (cont.)

Practice: Function Fun

1. Does the information in each table define a function? Why or why not?

A.
x	y
-5	-4
3	-4
0	-4
12	-4

_____
_____
_____
_____

B.
x	y
-1	-4
2	4
0	-5
0	-1

_____
_____
_____
_____

2. Graph the function described by the table entries provided.

x	y
-1	-4
3	4
0	-5
2	-1

3. A. Let $f(x) = \dfrac{x+1}{x-5}$

   B. Find $f(0)$: _____

   C. Find $f(35)$: _____

   D. If $f(x) = 7$, what was x? _____

4. A. Let $g(t) = 5 \cdot t + 4$

   B. Find $g(-4)$: _____

   C. Find $g(100)$: _____

   D. Find $g(b)$: _____

   E. Find $g(x + 3)$: _____

   F. If $g(t) = 39$, what was t? _____

Chapter 8: Functions (cont.)

Summary of Functions

A function can be defined most simply as a mathematical rule. A function provides the information necessary to pair an input number with an output number. A variable y is a function of a variable x if each value of x is assigned to exactly one value of y. The set of input values is called the domain, and the set of output values is called the range.

Tips to Remember

A function is a rule that pairs a number from one set with a number in a second set. It provides an input variable and an output variable. The output variable depends on the input variable.

A function sends every element of the first set (the domain) to exactly one element in the second set (the range).

Real Life Applications

Functions can be used to make graphs representing the relationship of two different variables.

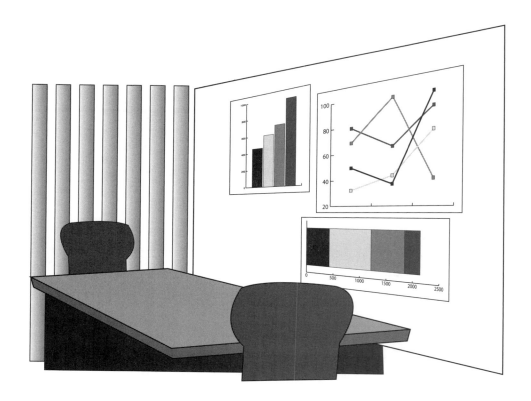

Chapter 9: Linear Functions

Introduction to Linear Functions

There are many types of functions. Certain relationships can be represented by function rules of the form, $f(x) = ax + b$, where a and b represent any real number. Function rules of this form are linear functions. This means that the graph of a linear function will be a line—easy to graph knowing two points that fall on the line. Many pairs of quantities vary in a linear way. For example, Celsius temperatures and Fahrenheit temperatures are linearly related. We can find a linear rule that allows us to input a Celsius temperature and get the equivalent Fahrenheit temperature as an output. The goal of this section is to review the basic forms of linear functions, how to write the equation for a line, and how to graph a line.

Concepts of Linear Functions

1 Standard Form

2 Graphing a Linear Function

3 Slope of a Line

4 Slope-Intercept Form

5 Point-Slope Form

6 Writing the Equation of a Line

    A Given Slope and y-intercept

    B Given Slope and Any Point

    C Given Two Points

Explanations of Concepts of Linear Functions

1 **Standard Form**

Linear functions all have the same standard form, $f(x) = mx + b$, where m and b can be any real numbers—fractions, decimals, irrational numbers, or integers. Examples of linear functions are given below. Notice all the different real numbers that can be a part of the equation.

$$f(x) = -3x + 5$$

$$g(x) = \frac{4}{5}x - 2$$

$$y = 0.35x + 0.78$$

$$f(t) = 2x + \sqrt{3}$$

Chapter 9: Linear Functions (cont.)

2 Graphing a Linear Function

The reason that functions of the form, $f(x) = mx + b$, are called linear is seen when these functions are graphed. How do we graph a linear function? The simplest way is to find at least two points (ordered pairs) that satisfy the rule and plot them on a coordinate plane.

For example, let's look at the graph of $f(x) = -3x + 5$. Let's build a table as we learned to do in the section on functions. Pick some input values and compute the related output values.

x	y
-1	-3(-1) + 5 = 8
3	-3(3) + 5 = -4
0	-3(0) + 5 = 5
2	-3(2) + 5 = -1

Now we have ordered pairs to plot and connect. Notice that each point falls along the same straight line. Also note the steepness of the line—it falls as the input values move from negative to positive.

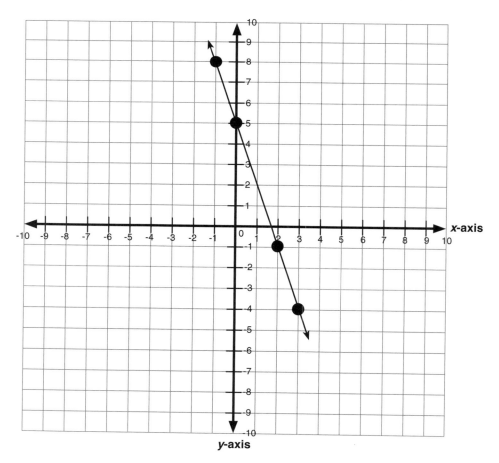

Chapter 9: Linear Functions (cont.)

3 Slope of a Line

The most important characteristic a line has is its steepness. Mathematically, we call the steepness of a line the **slope**. The number that describes the slope is easy to locate in the standard form of a line. The coefficient on the x term is the slope. In a function of the form, $f(x) = mx + b$, m is the coefficient on x and is the slope. In mathematics, the variable m is used to represent slope. It is important to know how to find the slope of a line. If you have the standard form for the line, you're set and know that the value of m is the slope. But what if you don't have the standard form? What if you only know two points that lie on the line? Can you find the slope? Yes, we find the slope by finding the ratio of change—comparing vertical change (change up and down) to horizontal change (change left to right). More commonly, we say that the slope is found by finding the $\dfrac{rise}{run} = \dfrac{y\text{-}change}{x\text{-}change}$. To find these changes, just do some subtraction. Suppose there are two points on a line, (x_1, y_1) and (x_2, y_2). To find the slope, take the difference in the y-coordinates and put it over the difference in the x-coordinates. This forms the ratio that measures the constant rate of change the line will have.

To find the slope of the line that passes through the two points (x_1, y_1) and (x_2, y_2):

$$slope = m = \frac{y_2 - y_1}{x_2 - x_1} = \frac{rise}{run}$$

Example:

Suppose the two points are: (-2, 2) and (4, -1). These two points determine a line. To find the slope for the line, find the differences—change in y over change in x.

$$slope = m = \frac{y_2 - y_1}{x_2 - x_1} = \frac{-1 - 2}{4 - -2} = \frac{-3}{6} = \frac{-1}{2}$$

The slope of the line will be $-\frac{1}{2}$. This ratio can be interpreted to mean for every unit you move down, move to the right 2 units. Plot the point (4, -1) and from that point move down one unit, over to the right 2 units, and place another point—it should be in line with the points (4, -1) and (-2, 2). Check it and see.

4 Slope-Intercept Form

The standard form, $f(x) = mx + b$, is also known as the slope-intercept form of a line. This is because the coefficient on the x term, m, is the slope of the line and the value b represents the y-intercept for the graph of the line—the point (0, b). With these two pieces of information from the equation, the slope and the y-intercept, the graph of the linear function can be produced.

101

Chapter 9: Linear Functions (cont.)

Let's look at an example.

Equation for linear function: $y = 3x + 2$.

This means that the slope of the line is $m = 3$, and the y-intercept is the point (0, 2).

We can think of the slope as $\dfrac{3}{1} = \dfrac{rise}{run} = \dfrac{vertical}{horizontal}$. Start by plotting the given y-intercept point (0, 2). Next, from that point, count up 3 units (the vertical change or rise) and then from the location, move 1 unit to the right (the horizontal change or run). This locates another point on the line. With these two points, you have determined the graph for the given linear function—connect and draw the arrows. Note that this process works if you are given any point on the line, not just the y-intercept. If you pick any point on the graphed line, AND move according to your slope, you should end up back on the line.

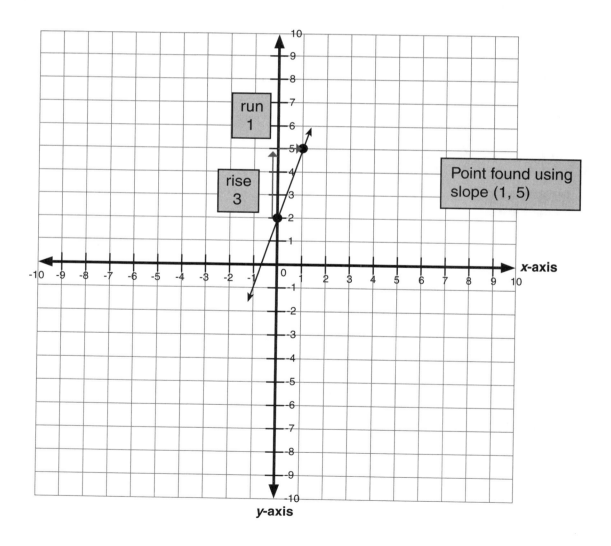

Chapter 9: Linear Functions (cont.)

5 Point-Slope Form

While the standard form or the slope-intercept form for a line is helpful—not all linear functions may be written in this form. Another form for a linear function is the point-slope form for a line. This form depends on knowing the slope of the line and any other point on the line —not necessarily the y-intercept. This provides more flexibility and will allow the writing of linear equations more efficiently.

Point-Slope Form

Let m be the slope of a line passing through the point (x_1, y_1). Then the equation of the line is given by: $y - y_1 = m(x - x_1)$.

Example:

The equation of the line with slope $m = \frac{4}{5}$ and passing through the point $(4, 11)$ is $y - 11 = \frac{4}{5}(x - 4)$.

Something to note is that if you simplify a linear equation in point-slope form using your algebra skills, you can put it into slope-intercept form. Let's try it with the equation created in the example above.

$$y - 11 = \frac{4}{5}(x - 4)$$

$$y - 11 = \frac{4}{5} \bullet x - \frac{4}{5} \bullet 4$$

$$y - 11 = \frac{4}{5}x - \frac{16}{5}$$

$$y - 11 + 11 = \frac{4}{5}x - \frac{16}{5} + 11$$

$$y = \frac{4}{5}x - \frac{16}{5} + \frac{55}{5}$$

$$y = \frac{4}{5}x - \frac{39}{5}$$

This indicates that the y-intercept is $\left(0, -\frac{39}{5}\right)$ with a slope of $\frac{4}{5}$.

Chapter 9: Linear Functions (cont.)

6 Writing the Equation of a Line

The equation of a linear function can be written if (A.) the slope and y-intercept are given; (B.) the slope and any point are given; or (C.) any two points on the line are given.

A Given the slope and y-intercept

Example: Let the slope = m = -5 and the y-intercept be (0, 3)
Use the slope-intercept form of a line, $y = mx + b$, and substitute to get the equation $y = -5x + 3$.

B Given the slope and any point on the line

Example: Let the slope = m = 0.75 and the point be (0.5, 6).
Use the point-slope form of a line, $y - y_1 = m(x - x_1)$ and substitute to get the equation $y - 6 = 0.75(x - 0.5)$. It is fine to leave the equation in this form unless you are asked to simplify it into slope-intercept form.

C Given two points on the line

Example: Let the two points given be (3, -2) and (5, 7). Note that in this case the slope is not given. Can the slope be found? Yes.

$$m = \frac{y_2 - y_1}{x_2 - x_1} = \frac{7 - -2}{5 - 3} = \frac{9}{2} = 4\frac{1}{2}$$

Now, since the slope is known, pick one of the two points given. Either one will work—they are both on the line. Then, follow the process of the previous example to use the point-slope form of a linear equation to get the needed equation.

$$y - 7 = 4.5(x - 5)$$

Again, leave it in this form unless asked to put your answer in slope-intercept form.

Chapter 9: Linear Functions (cont.)

Practice: Learning the Lines

1. For each linear function below, identify the slope and the y-intercept.

    A. $f(x) = -3x + 5$ slope = _____ and y-intercept = _____

    B. $g(x) = \frac{4}{5}x - 2$ slope = _____ and y-intercept = _____

    C. $y = 0.35x + 0.78$ slope = _____ and y-intercept = _____

    D. $f(t) = 2x + \sqrt{3}$ slope = _____ and y-intercept = _____

2. Graph each of the linear functions below on your own paper by completing a table and plotting the points on a coordinate plane.

    A. $f(x) = 3x + 2$ B. $g(x) = 3x - 5$

    C. $h(x) = -\frac{1}{3}x + \frac{7}{3}$ D. $k(x) = 0.5x + 4.5$

    After graphing your lines, answer the following on your own paper.

    E. How would you describe the relationship between the graph of $f(x)$ and $g(x)$?

    F. What is the slope of $f(x)$? $g(x)$?

    G. How would you describe the relationship between the graph of $g(x)$ and $h(x)$?

    H. What is the slope of $g(x)$? $h(x)$?

3. Write the equation for the line that satisfies the given information.

    A. slope = $\frac{3}{4}$ and y-intercept = 6 _____

    B. slope = -11 and through the point (5, 7) _____

    C. through the points (-3, 9) and (5, -5) _____

    D. through the points (4, 7) and (-6, -6) and put into slope-intercept form

    _____

4. In Celsius temperature, freezing occurs at 0° and boiling at 100°. On the Fahrenheit scale, freezing occurs at 32° and boiling at 212°. On your own paper, form two ordered pairs of the form (C, F) for the freezing and boiling points of liquids. Using these two points, find a linear equation for converting Celsius temperatures to their equivalent Fahrenheit temperatures. Using your equation, what is the Fahrenheit temperature if it is 55° Celsius?

_____

Chapter 9: Linear Functions (cont.)

Summary of Linear Functions

Linear functions all have the same standard form, $f(x) = ax + b$, where a and b can be any real numbers—fractions, decimals, irrational numbers, or integers will work. There are many ways to find and write the functional equation for a line including slope-intercept form and point-slope form. The equation for a line is completely determined by any two points that fall on the line. Graphing a linear function is as simple as choosing any two input values for x and solving for the output, or y values. The most important characteristic of a line is the slope or steepness of the line.

Tips to Remember

Lines with positive slope rise from left to right, and lines with negative slope fall from left to right. Parallel lines have equal slopes, and two lines that are perpendicular will have slopes that are negative reciprocals of each other.

Real Life Applications of Linear Functions

Many quantities are related in a linear way. If we count cricket chirps per minute, we find a linear relationship to the air temperature. We can use the number of cricket chirps to find the current air temperature. Another example used in everyday life is in the area of measurement conversion—moving from the Celsius scale to the Fahrenheit temperature scale or vice versa. We can find a linear function that will allow conversion in either direction.

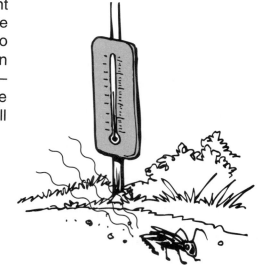

Chapter 10: Quadratic Functions

Introduction to Quadratic Functions

There are a variety of functions that can be used to describe relationships between two variables. In this section, the group of functions called quadratic functions will be investigated. These second-degree polynomial functions are useful in describing real-world phenomena, like the path that a ball makes if it is thrown straight up into the air. Perhaps the most visual illustration of a quadratic function in action in the real world is the Gateway Arch in St. Louis, Missouri. The graph or visual illustration of a quadratic function will always turn out to be a parabola. For this reason, quadratic functions are sometimes referred to as parabolic functions. To be able to graph quadratic equations efficiently, the important characteristics of the parabola will be identified and a formula presented for finding the most important point on the parabola, the vertex.

Concepts of Quadratic Functions

1 General Form of a Quadratic Function

2 Graphing a Quadratic Function

    A Parabola

    B Vertex

Explanation of Concepts of Quadratic Functions

1 General Form of a Quadratic Function

Just as linear functions all have the same general form, the next class of functions called quadratic functions will all have the same general form. A function is called quadratic if it is of the form, $f(x) = ax^2 + bx + c$, where a, b, and c are real numbers and $a \neq 0$. Because of the exponent on the lead term, ax^2, quadratic functions are degree two polynomial functions.

Examples of Quadratic Functions:

$$f(x) = x^2 + 3x + 4$$

$$g(t) = -2t^2 + 7$$

$$h(x) = \tfrac{2}{3}x^2 + 6x$$

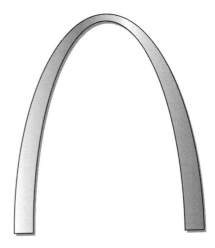

Chapter 10: Quadratic Functions (cont.)

2 Graphing a Quadratic Function

One approach to graphing a quadratic function is to set up a table, pick some inputs for x, and compute the related outputs. Then take your ordered pairs from the table and plot them on the coordinate system and connect the points to form the graph. For example, suppose we want to graph the quadratic function, $f(x) = x^2$. The table below shows one choice of ordered pairs that could be used to sketch the graph of the function.

x	y
-1	1
2	4
0	0
1	1

A Parabola

The resulting graph of the quadratic function reveals a shape called a **parabola**. It is easy to tell whether the graph of a quadratic function, $f(x) = ax^2 + bx + c$, will be a parabola opening up or opening down. Look at the coefficient a of the ax^2 term of the function rule. If a is positive, the parabola opens up (holding water like a bowl), and if a is negative, the parabola opens down (shedding water like an umbrella).

So, the graph of $g(x) = -x^2$ is the mirror image of $f(x) = x^2$. It is the same parabola, just opening down rather than opening up as is seen in the figure below.

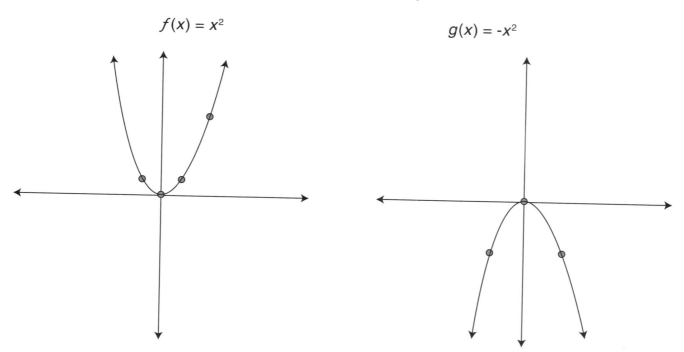

$f(x) = x^2$ $g(x) = -x^2$

Chapter 10: Quadratic Functions (cont.)

What other information can a, the coefficient on the ax^2 term, provide? To investigate, let's graph three different quadratic functions on the same coordinate system and look to see what happens. For this example, the functions to graph are:

$$f(x) = x^2 \qquad\qquad g(x) = 2x^2 \qquad\qquad h(x) = \tfrac{1}{2}x^2$$

By plotting the points shown, the graphs of the three functions are as seen.

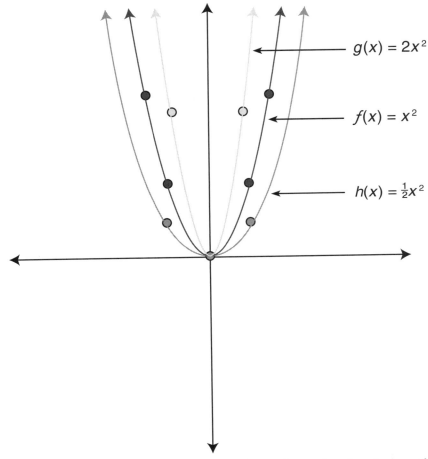

Let's consider the graph of the function $f(x) = x^2$ as the basic parabola. How does putting a 2 as the coefficient on x^2 change the basic parabola? Since the graph of $g(x)$ falls inside our basic parabola, the 2 has made the parabola narrower. What about using a value for the coefficient that is less than one, like $\tfrac{1}{2}$? Note that the graph of $h(x)$ falls outside of the basic parabola. The fractional value causes the parabola to widen or broaden from the basic x^2 shape. The role of a, the coefficient on x^2, tells two valuable pieces of information for graphing a quadratic function of the form, $f(x) = ax^2 + bx + c$. One, if $a > 0$, then the parabola will open up, and if $a < 0$, the parabola will open down. Second, if $a > 1$, the parabola will be narrower than the general x^2 parabola, and if $0 < a < 1$, the parabola will be wider than the general x^2 parabola.

109

Chapter 10: Quadratic Functions (cont.)

Examples:

Function	Parabola opens	Narrow or Wide
$f(x) = -5x^2 + 7$	DOWN	NARROW
$g(t) = 0.25t^2 - 5t + 3$	UP	WIDE

B   **Vertex**

Now that several examples of simple quadratic functions have been seen and it is clear what a parabola looks like, what other important characteristic would it be helpful to have to quickly and efficiently draw the graph of a quadratic function? How about knowing the high point or maximum height for the graph (if the parabola opens down) or the low point or minimum height for the graph (if the parabola opens up). Wouldn't that make graphing a parabola easier? It turns out that we can find this point called the vertex of the parabola.

The vertex of the parabola defined by the quadratic function of the form, $f(x) = ax^2 + bx + c$, where a, b, and c are real numbers and $a \neq 0$, is found at the point $\left(\frac{-b}{2a}, \ f\left(\frac{-b}{2a}\right) \right)$.
So, based on the coefficients for the x^2 and x terms, we can determine the x-coordinate for the vertex and then evaluate the function for that value of x to get the y-coordinate for the vertex.

Example:

Step 1: Consider the quadratic function, $f(x) = -2x^2 + 6x + 1$. Find the vertex.

Step 2: The x-coordinate is $\dfrac{-6}{2(-2)} = \dfrac{-6}{-4} = \dfrac{3}{2} = 1\dfrac{1}{2}$

because $a = -2$ and $b = 6$.

Step 3: The y-coordinate is $f(1.5) = -2(1.5)^2 + 6(1.5) + 1 = 5.5$

Step 4: The vertex for the parabola will be at the point (1.5, 5.5). Note the parabola will open down from this point, since the coefficient on x^2 is a -2.

To complete the graph of a quadratic function, it is helpful to find the x-intercept(s) and the y-intercept for the graph. Start with the y-intercept. To find the y-intercept for the function, $f(x) = ax^2 + bx + c$, let $x = 0$, and find the value for $f(0)$. Note that this will always be the value c! This means that the point $(0, c)$ will be a point on the graph of the parabola.

The graph of a quadratic function might not intersect the x-axis at all, it might touch at one point (think of $f(x) = x^2$ touching only at (0, 0)), or it might intersect the x-axis at two points.

Chapter 10: Quadratic Functions (cont.)

To find the *x*-intercept or *x*-intercepts for the graph of $f(x) = ax^2 + bx + c$, we can use what we learned about solving quadratic equations. Namely, we can use factoring or the Quadratic Formula to locate the *x*-intercept value or values. To do this, set the given quadratic function equal to 0 and solve for *x*.

Example:

Problem: $f(x) = x^2 + x - 12$

Step 1: Find the *y*-intercept: Let $x = 0$, find $f(0) = 0^2 + 0 - 12 = -12$, so the point (0, -12) is on the parabola.

Step 2: Find the *x*-intercept: Let $y = f(x) = 0$ and solve for *x*.

$0 = x^2 + x - 12$ Try factoring as the first method of solution.

$0 = (x - 3)(x + 4)$

$0 = x - 3$ or $0 = x + 4$

$x = 3$ or $x = -4$

This means that the parabola will intersect the *x*-axis in two points (3, 0) and (-4, 0).

Step 3: What would the vertex for this parabola be? $x = -\frac{1}{2}$

(by substitution in $x = -\frac{b}{2a}$).

Step 4: And $f(-\frac{1}{2}) = (-\frac{1}{2})^2 + (-\frac{1}{2}) - 12 = -\frac{49}{4}$, so the vertex point is $(-\frac{1}{2}, -\frac{49}{4})$.

Step 5: Does the parabola open up or down? Up, because the coefficient on x^2 is positive.

Step 6: All of this information can now be used to draw the graph for the quadratic function in the example.

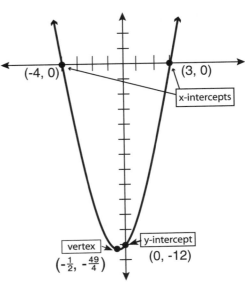

Name: _____ Date: _____

Chapter 10: Quadratic Functions (cont.)

Practice: Quadratic Functions—Parabola Practice Makes Perfect

1. Complete the table below:

	Function	Parabola Opens	Narrow or Wide
A.	$f(t) = -3t^2 - 7$		
B.	$g(x) = 7x^2 + 3x$		
C.	$h(x) = 0.56x^2 + 0.4x - 1$		

2. For each quadratic function below, find the vertex for the parabola.

   A. $f(x) = 2x^2 - 7x - 4$ _____

   B. $g(t) = 6t^2 + 3t$ _____

   C. $h(x) = x^2 - 9x + 2$ _____

3. For each quadratic function, find the x-intercepts, if they exist.

   A. $f(x) = 2x^2 - 7x - 4$ _____

   B. $g(t) = 6t^2 + 3t$ _____

   C. $h(x) = x^2 - 9x + 2$ _____

4. Using your own graph paper, graph the function given by $f(x) = 2x^2 - 7x - 4$.

Chapter 10: Quadratic Functions (cont.)

Summary of Quadratic Functions

A function is called quadratic if it is of the form, $f(x) = ax^2 + bx + c$, where a, b, and c are real numbers and $a \neq 0$. To be able to graph a quadratic equation of the form $f(x) = ax^2 + bx + c$ efficiently, the important characteristics of the parabola need to be identified and used.

- If $a > 0$, then the parabola will open up.

- If $a < 0$, the parabola will open down.

- If $a > 1$, the parabola will be narrower than the general x^2 parabola.

- If $0 < a < 1$, the parabola will be wider than the general x^2 parabola.

- The vertex of the parabola is found at the point $\left(\dfrac{-b}{2a}, \ f\left(\dfrac{-b}{2a} \right) \right)$.

- To find the y-intercept: Let $x = 0$, find $f(0)$. Plot the point $(0, f(0))$.

- To find the x-intercept: Let $y = f(x) = 0$ and solve for x. Use either factoring or the Quadratic Formula to find x.

Putting all this information together will provide the graph for the given quadratic function.

Tips to Remember

It is easy to tell whether the graph of a quadratic function, $f(x) = ax^2 + bx + c$, will be a parabola opening up or opening down. Look at the coefficient a of the ax^2 term of the function rule. If a is positive, the parabola opens up, and if a is negative, the parabola opens down.

Real Life Applications of Quadratic Functions

Quadratic functions are used to describe many phenomena that occur in the world. For example, if a ball is thrown into the air, it follows a parabolic path. The equation that describes the impact of gravity on falling objects is quadratic in form. Perhaps the most visual illustration of a quadratic function in action in the real world is the Gateway Arch in St. Louis, Missouri.

Answer Keys

Chapter 2: Review of Properties Practice Page (p. 21)

		Simplify	Property
1.	$x + 0$	x	Identity Property of Addition
2.	$b \cdot 1 =$	b	Identity Property of Multiplication
3.	$\frac{1}{5} \cdot 0 = 0 \cdot \frac{1}{5}$	0	Commutative Property of Multiplication
4.	$3y \cdot 7 = 7 \cdot 3y$	$21y = 21y$	Commutative Property of Multiplication
5.	$a + b = b + a$	$a + b = b + a$	Commutative Property of Addition
6.	$(3 + 9) + 7 = 3 + (9 + 7)$	$19 = 19$	Associative Property of Addition
7.	$5 \cdot x$ and $\frac{5x}{5} =$	x	Inverse Operations
8.	$(d \cdot b) \cdot c = d \cdot (b \cdot c)$	$dbc = dbc$	Associative Property of Multiplication
9.	$x - 7 + 7 =$	x	Inverse Operations
10.	$3(5 + 2) = 3 \cdot 5 + 3 \cdot 2$	$21 = 21$	Distributive Property of Multiplication Over Addition
11.	$a(b + c) = a \cdot b + a \cdot c$	$a(b + c) = ab + ac$	Distributive Property of Multiplication Over Addition
12.	$a \cdot \frac{1}{a} =$	1	Reciprocal/Multiplicative Inverse

Chapter 3: Practice with Exponents and Exponential Expressions (p. 31–32)

1. $10^2 = 100$
2. $6^{10} = 60{,}466{,}176$
3. $y^0 = 1$ Any variable raised to the ^{0} power is 1.
4. $5(-3)^3 = 5(-27) = -135$
5. $10(b)^2 = 10(b^2) = 10b^2$
6. $10(z^3) + 2(z^3)$ $10 + 2 = 12$ so $10(z^3) + 2(z^3) = 12(z^3)$
7. $5(z^3) - 3(z^3)$ $5 - 3 = 2$, so $5(z^3) - 3(z^3) = 2(z^3)$
8. $3(z^3) - 1(z)$ Exponents are not the same, so it cannot be subtracted.
9. $(z^3)(z^4)$ $3 + 4 = 7$ $(z^3)(z^4) = z^7$
10. $(c^3)(c^2)$ $3 + 2 = 5$ $(c^3)(c^2) = c^5$
11. $(6x^4)(3x^2)$ $(6)(3) = 18$ $4 + 2 = 6$ $= 18x^6$
12. $3^2 \div 3$ Both roots are 3. $2 - 1 = 1$ $3^2 \div 3 = 3^1 = 3$
13. $x^4 \div x^2$ Both roots are x. $4 - 2 = 2$ $x^4 \div x^2 = x^2$
14. $\frac{5^2}{1^3}$ Different roots cannot divide
15. $(7^2)^0$ $2 \times 0 = 0$ $(7^2)^0 = 7^0 = 1$ Any number raised to the ^{0} power = 1.
16. $(x^4)^2$ $4 \times 2 = 8$ $(x^4)^2 = x^8$
17. $(5y^3)^3$ $3 \times 3 = 9$ $(5y^3)^3 = 5^3 y^9 = 125y^9$
18. 5^{-4} $5 = \frac{5}{1}$ the reciprocal $= \frac{1}{5}$, $5^{-4} = \frac{1}{5^4}$
19. 2^{-6} $2 = \frac{2}{1}$, the reciprocal $= \frac{1}{2}$, $2^{-6} = \frac{1}{2^6}$
20. $\left(\frac{1}{a}\right)^{-3}$ $\frac{1}{a}$, the reciprocal $= \frac{a}{1}$, $\left(\frac{1}{a}\right)^{-3} = a^3$

Chapter 4: Practice: Roots and Radicals (p. 41–42)

1. $\sqrt{4}$ 2   Perfect Square

2. $\sqrt{9}$ 3   Perfect Square

3. $\sqrt{1}$ 1   Perfect Square

4. $\sqrt{3}$ 1.732050808   Not a perfect Square

5. $\sqrt{2}$ 1.414213562   Not a perfect Square

6. $\sqrt{(25)(9)}$ $(\sqrt{25})(\sqrt{9}) = (5)(3) = 15$

7. $\sqrt{(4)(16)}$ $(\sqrt{4})(\sqrt{16}) = (2)(4) = 8$

8. $\sqrt{16y^2}$ $y > 0 \ (\sqrt{16})(\sqrt{y^2}) = (4)(y) = 4y$

9. $(\sqrt{y})(\sqrt{y})$ $y > 0 \ \sqrt{(y)(y)} = \sqrt{y^2} = y$

10. $(\sqrt{3})(\sqrt{12})$ $\sqrt{(3)(12)} = \sqrt{36} = 6$

11. $\sqrt{32} = \sqrt{(2)(16)} = (\sqrt{2})(\sqrt{16}) = (\sqrt{2})(4) \approx (1.414213562)(4) \approx 5.656854249$

12. $\sqrt{125} = (\sqrt{5})(\sqrt{25}) = (\sqrt{5})(5) = 2.236067978\,(5) = 11.18033989$

13. $\sqrt{\dfrac{25}{36}} = \dfrac{\sqrt{25}}{\sqrt{36}} = \dfrac{5}{6}$

14. $\sqrt{\dfrac{64}{16}} = \dfrac{\sqrt{64}}{\sqrt{16}} = \dfrac{8}{4} = 2$

15. $\sqrt{\dfrac{4}{3}} = \dfrac{\sqrt{4}}{\sqrt{3}} = (\dfrac{2}{\sqrt{3}})(\dfrac{\sqrt{3}}{\sqrt{3}}) = \dfrac{2\sqrt{3}}{\sqrt{3}\,(3)} = \dfrac{2\sqrt{3}}{\sqrt{9}} = \dfrac{2\sqrt{3}}{3}$

16. $3\sqrt{36} + \sqrt{1}$ Different numbers under the radical signs. Cannot be added.

17. $4\sqrt[5]{x} + 5\sqrt[5]{x}$ $4 + 5 = 9$ $= 9\sqrt[5]{x}$

18. $6\sqrt[5]{x} + \sqrt[2]{x}$ Indexes are different. Cannot be added.

19. $8\sqrt{5} - 4\sqrt{5}$ $8 - 4 = 4$ $= 4\sqrt{5}$

20. $9\sqrt{2y} - 3\sqrt{2y}$ $9 - 3 = 6$ $= 6\sqrt{2y}$

21. $\sqrt[3]{8}$ 2 $2 \times 2 \times 2 = 8$

22. $\sqrt[3]{27}$ 3 $3 \times 3 \times 3 = 27$

23. $\sqrt[6]{64}$ 2 $2 \times 2 \times 2 \times 2 \times 2 \times 2 = 64$

24. $\sqrt[9]{1}$ 1 $1 \times 1 \times 1 \times 1 \times 1 \times 1 \times 1 \times 1 \times 1 = 1$

25. $\sqrt[4]{-81}$ Index is even number, cannot be solved.

26. $\sqrt[3]{-1}$ Index is odd: $-1 \times -1 \times -1 = -1$

27. $\sqrt{-4}$ Index is even number, cannot be solved.

28. $\sqrt[5]{a^2}$ $a^{\frac{Exponent}{Index}} = a^{\frac{2}{5}}$

29. $\sqrt{7}$ Square root, so index is 2, and exponent is 1: $7^{\frac{Exponent}{Index}}$ or $7^{\frac{1}{2}}$

30. $b^{\frac{2}{3}}$ $\sqrt[3]{b^2}$

31. $(5y)^{\frac{1}{3}}$ $\sqrt[3]{5y}$

32. $10^{\frac{1}{2}}$ $\sqrt{10}$

Chapter 5: Practice: Operations on Algebraic Expressions (p. 55–56)

1. $335 + 1{,}567 = 1{,}902$
2. $3a + 24b + 4c = ?$ Unlike terms cannot be added.
3. $\frac{1}{2}x + 5x = 5\frac{1}{2}x$
4. $4x - 8y = ?$ Unlike terms cannot be subtracted.
5. $7 - \frac{1}{2} = 6\frac{1}{2}$
6. $7y \cdot 8z = 56yz$
7. $10a \cdot 35a = 350a^2$
8. $\frac{3}{8} \div \frac{1}{8} = 3$
9. $\frac{300}{25} = 12$
10. $35x \div 7xy = \frac{5}{y}$
11. $\frac{8ab}{b} = 8a$
12. $5 - -3 = 5 + 3 = 8$
13. $|0| = 0$
14. $|-21| = 21$
15. $15 - -8 = 23$
16. $20 \times -5 = -100$
17. $100 \div -10 = -10$
18. $-36 \div 6 = -6$
19. $-3(6 + -2) = -12$
20. $12 \div -6 + 4 - -7 = (12 \div -6) + 4 - -7 = -2 + 4 - -7 = 2 - -7 = 2 + 7 = 9$
21. $0 + y = y$

22. $0 - 13 =$ -13
23. $0 - (-12) = 12$
24. $8xyz \cdot 0 = 0$
25. $0 \div f = 0$
26. $3 \div 0 = ?$ Cannot divide by 0.
27. $-7n \cdot 5y^2 = -35ny^2$
28. $\dfrac{16b^2}{2b} = 8b$
29. $17t - 3t + 9t = 23t$
30. $21x + \frac{3}{4}x = 21\frac{3}{4}x$

Chapter 5: Practice: All Numbers, All Signs, Let's Operate! (p. 60)

1. $\frac{3}{-5} \times \frac{7}{8} = \frac{21}{-40}$
2. $7.8 + -5.3 = 2.5$
3. $-110 \div 2.5 = -44$
4. $5\sqrt{3} + -11\sqrt{3} = -6\sqrt{3} \approx -10.392$
5. $-2.3 \times -10.2 = 23.46$
6. $5 \times -36 = -180$
7. $\frac{2}{-3} + \frac{5}{6} = \frac{4}{-6} + \frac{5}{6} = \frac{1}{6}$
8. $\frac{10}{-11} \div \frac{15}{22} = \frac{10}{-11} \times \frac{22}{15} = \frac{2}{-1} \times \frac{2}{3} = \frac{4}{-3} = -1\frac{1}{3}$
9. $2(4.7 + -3.6) = 2.2$
10. $|-7 - -3.5| = 3.5$
11. $8\sqrt{2} + -6\sqrt{2} = 2\sqrt{2} \approx 2.828$
12. $-3.71 - -4.2 = 0.49$
13. $\frac{9}{10} - \frac{2}{-5} = \frac{9}{10} - \frac{4}{-10} = \frac{13}{10} = 1\frac{3}{10}$
14. $-18.5 + 17.2 = -1.3$
15. $-6.3 \times -10.3 = 64.89$

Chapter 6: Practice: Equations and Problem Solving (p. 83)

1. $x(5x + 8) = 0$ $5x^2 + 8x = 0$
2. $-a(10a - 2) = 0$ $-10a^2 + 2a = 0$
3. $4x(2x - 3) = -3$ $8x^2 - 12x = -3$
4. $(2c - 5)(3c + 1) = 0$ $6c^2 + 2c - 15c - 5 = 0$ $6c^2 - 13c - 5 = 0$
5. $(x + 2)(x - 3) = 0$ $x^2 - 3x + 2x - 6 = 0$ $x^2 - 1x - 6 = 0$
6. $3x^2 - 27 = 0$ $x = 3$ or -3
7. $2a^2 - 6a = 0$ $a = 0$ or 3
8. $2b^2 + 7b = -6$ $b = -2$ or $-\frac{3}{2}$
9. $x^2 + 6x + 7 = 0$ $t = -3 + \sqrt{2}$ or $t = -3 - \sqrt{2}$
10. $2x^2 + 5x + 2 = 0$ $x = -2$ or $-\frac{1}{2}$
11. $3x^2 + x - 2 = 0$ $x = -1$ or $\frac{2}{3}$
12. The dimensions of the dog pen are 4 meters by 12 meters or 6 meters by 8 meters.
13. $18x^3 + 66x^2 - 24x = 0$ $\{0, -4, \frac{1}{3}\}$
14. $ax - ay - bx + by$ ⌉ $(x - y)(a - b)$ $a - b = 0$
    $a(x - y) - b(x - y)$ $x - y = 0$ $a - b + b = 0 + b$
    $\dfrac{a(x - \cancel{y}) - b(x - \cancel{y})}{(\cancel{x - y}) \quad (\cancel{x - y})}$ ⌋ $x - y + y = 0 + y$ $a = b$
              $x = y$

15. $\dfrac{b-2}{15} = \dfrac{2}{5}$ $b = 8$

16. $\dfrac{3}{x+2} - \dfrac{1}{x} = \dfrac{1}{5x}$ $x = \dfrac{4}{3}$

Chapter 7: Graphing Practice: Orderly Ordered Pairs (p. 89)

1. Quadrant II
2. There are many possible answers, but pair should look like (positive number, negative number).
3. If connected correctly, should spell MATH. Group 1 forms the M, Group 2 forms the A, Groups 3 and 4 together form the T, and Groups 5, 6, and 7 together form the H.

Chapter 8: Function Practice: Function Fun (p. 97)

1. Does the information in each table define a function? Why or Why not?

x	y
-5	-4
3	-4
0	-4
12	-4

x	y
-1	-4
2	4
0	-5
0	-1

YES – each x is paired with only one output value – even if it is the same for all inputs. This is called a constant function.

NO – 0 is being paired with both -5 and -1 as outputs

2. Graph the function described by the table entries provided:

x	y
-1	-4
3	4
0	-5
2	-1

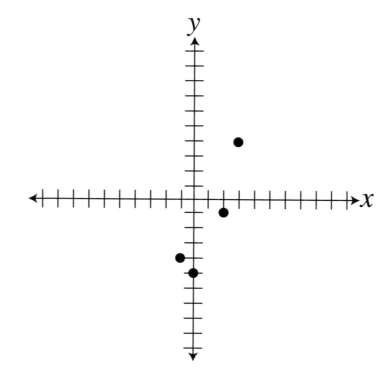

3. A.   Let $f(x) = \dfrac{x+1}{x-5}$

    B.   Find $f(0)$: $f(0) = \dfrac{0+1}{0-5} = -\dfrac{1}{5}$

    C.   Find $f(35)$: $f(35) = \dfrac{35+1}{35-5} = \dfrac{36}{30} = \dfrac{6}{5} = 1\dfrac{1}{5}$

    D.   If $f(x) = 7$, what was x?

          $7 = \dfrac{x+1}{x-5}$ and then solve for x. Begin by multiplying both sides by $x - 5$:

          $7(x - 5) = x + 1$
          $7x - 35 = x + 1$
          $7x = x + 1 + 35$
          $7x - x = 36$
          $6x = 36$
          $x = 6$

4. A.   Let $g(t) = 5 \bullet t + 4$
    B.   Find $g(-4)$: $g(-4) = 5 \bullet -4 + 4 = -20 + 4 = -16$
    C.   Find $g(100)$: $g(100) = 5 \bullet 100 + 4 = 500 + 4 = 504$
    D.   Find $g(b)$: $g(b) = 5 \bullet b + 4$
    E.   Find $g(x + 3)$: $g(x + 3) = 5(x + 3) + 4 = 5x + 15 + 4 = 5x + 19$
    F.   If $g(t) = 39$, what was t?
          $39 = 5 \bullet t + 4$
          $39 - 4 = 5 \bullet t + 4 - 4$
          $35 = 5t$
          $\dfrac{35}{5} = \dfrac{5t}{5}$
          $7 = t$

Chapter 9: Linear Functions Practice: Learning the Lines (p. 105)

1. For each linear function below, identify the slope and the y-intercept:

    $f(x) = -3x + 5$ slope = -3 and y-intercept = 5
    $g(x) = \frac{4}{5}x - 2$ slope = $\frac{4}{5}$ and y-intercept = -2
    $y = 0.35x + 0.78$ slope = 0.35 and y-intercept = 0.78
    $f(t) = 2x + \sqrt{3}$ slope = 2 and y-intercept = $\sqrt{3}$

2. The tables shown are examples. Answers will differ depending on the choice of x values. It is always a good idea to plot at least three points to check and make sure they all fall on the same straight line. If you see that they don't, then check your math for errors.

A.

x	$f(x)$
-1	-1
2	8
0	2

B.

x	$g(x)$
0	-5
1	-2
3	4

C.

x	$h(x)$
0	$2\frac{1}{3}$
1	2
6	$\frac{1}{3}$

D.

x	$k(x)$
0	4.5
1	5
-5	2

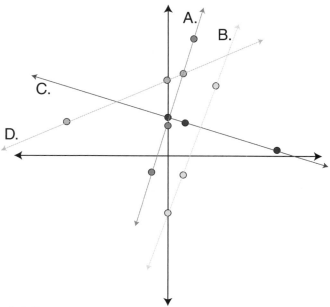

E. They are parallel lines.

F. Both lines have a slope of 3. Parallel lines will always have the same slope.

G. They are perpendicular lines.

H. 3, $-\frac{1}{3}$ Lines that are perpendicular will always have slopes that are negative reciprocals of one another. In this case, the reciprocal of 3 is $\frac{1}{3}$, and the negative of that is $-\frac{1}{3}$.

3. A. slope = $\frac{3}{4}$ and y-intercept = 6

Since $y = mx + b$ is the slope-intercept form, substitute $\frac{3}{4}$ for m and 6 for b to get: $y = \frac{3}{4} m + 6$

B. slope = -11 and through the point (5, 7)

For this equation, use the point-slope form of a line, substitute -11 for m and use 5 for x_1 and 7 for y_1. The equation needed is $y - 7 = -11(x - 5)$.

C. Through the points (-3, 9) and (5, -5)

First, find the slope $\frac{-5 - 9}{5 - -3} = \frac{-14}{8}$. Next, use the point-slope form to write the equation, $y - y_1 = m(x - x_1)$ using the slope found and one of the two points given to get the equation, $y - 9 = -\frac{14}{8} (x + 3)$.

D. through the points (4, 7) and (-6, -6), put into slope-intercept form.

Find the slope, $\frac{13}{10}$ using the slope formula. Choose one of the two points, for example, (4, 7). Now substitute into the point-slope form to get

$y - 7 = \frac{13}{10} (x - 4)$ and then use algebra to simplify and solve for y.

$y - 7 = \frac{13}{10} x - \frac{13}{10}(4)$

$y - 7 = \frac{13}{10}x - \frac{25}{6}$

$y = \frac{13}{10}x - \frac{25}{6} + 7$

$y = \frac{13}{10}x - \frac{25}{6} + \frac{35}{5}$

$y = \frac{13}{10}x + \frac{9}{5}$

4. The two points of form (C, F) are (0, 32) and (100, 212).
   Find the slope using the points:

   $$m = \frac{212 - 32}{100 - 0} = \frac{180}{100} = \frac{9}{5}$$

   Next, notice that the point (0, 32) is the *y*-intercept point for the line.
   Use the slope-intercept form to write the needed equation:

   $$F = \frac{9}{5}C + 32$$

   Now, input C = 55 and solve for F.

   $$F = \frac{9}{5} \bullet 55 + 32 = 99 + 32 = 131$$

   When the Celsius temperature is 55°, the Fahrenheit scale would read 131°.

Chapter Practice: Quadratic Functions—Parabola Practice Makes Perfect (p. 112)

1. Complete the table below:

Function	Parabola Opens	Narrow or Wide
A. $f(t) = -3t^2 - 7$	Down	Narrow
B. $g(x) = 7x^2 + 3x$	Up	Narrow
C. $h(x) = 0.56x^2 + 0.4x - 1$	Up	Wide

2. For each quadratic function below, find the vertex for the parabola.

   A. $f(x) = -2x^2 - 7x - 4$ Vertex: $\left(\frac{7}{4}, -10\frac{1}{8}\right)$ *or* (1.75, -10.125)

   B. $g(t) = 6t^2 + 3t$ Vertex: $\left(-\frac{1}{4}, -\frac{3}{8}\right)$ *or* (-0.25, -0.375)

   C. $h(x) = x^2 - 9x + 2$ Vertex: $\left(\frac{9}{2}, -18\frac{1}{4}\right)$ *or* (4.5, -18.25)

3. For each quadratic function, find the *x*-intercepts, if they exist.
   A. $f(x) = 2x^2 - 7x - 4$
      Use factoring: $2x^2 - 7x - 4 = 0$
      $$(2x + 1)(x - 4) = 0$$
      $$2x + 1 = 0 \quad or \quad x - 4 = 0$$
      $$2x = -1 \qquad\qquad x = 4$$
      $$x = -\frac{1}{2}$$
   So, $(-\frac{1}{2}, 0)$ and (4, 0) are the *x*-intercepts for the parabola.
   B. $g(t) = 6t^2 + 3t$
      Use factoring: $6t^2 + 3t = 0$
      $$3t(2t + 1) = 0$$
      $$3t = 0 \qquad\qquad or \qquad\qquad 2t + 1 = 0$$
      $$t = 0 \qquad\qquad\qquad\qquad 2t = -1$$
      $$t = -\frac{1}{2}$$
   So, (0, 0) and $(-\frac{1}{2}, 0)$ are the *x*-intercepts for the parabola.

C. $h(x) = x^2 - 9x + 2$

Factoring won't work on this function. Use the Quadratic Formula:

Note $a = 1$, $b = -9$, and $c = 2$

$$x = \frac{-b \pm \sqrt{b^2 - 4ac}}{2a}$$

$$= \frac{-(-9) \pm \sqrt{(-9)^2 - 4(1)(2)}}{2(1)}$$

$$= \frac{9 \pm \sqrt{81 - 8}}{2}$$

$$x = \frac{9 + \sqrt{73}}{2} \approx 8.77$$

or $x = \frac{9 - \sqrt{73}}{2} \approx 0.23$

So, (8.77, 0) and (0.23, 0) are the x-intercepts for the parabola.

4. Graph function given by $f(x) = 2x^2 - 7x - 4$.

Use the information in Problems #2A and #3A.

The graph should have a parabola that opens up and is narrower than the x^2 parabola.

Vertex: (1.75, -10.125)

$(-\frac{1}{2}, 0)$ and (4, 0) are the x-intercepts for the parabola.

In addition, the point (0, -4) is on the graph. It is the y-intercept of the parabola.

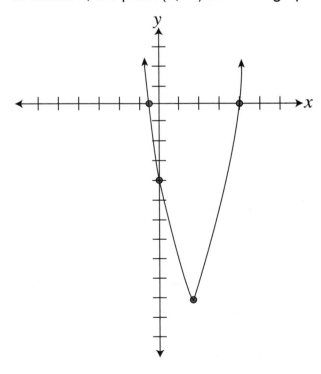

References

References

Brown, R., Dolciani, M., Sorgenfrey, R., Cole,W., (1997). *Algebra Structure and Method Book.* Evanston, IL: McDougal Littell.

Chicago Mathematics Project . *Connected Mathematics.* University of Chicago. Found online at: http://www.math.msu.edu/cmp/curriculum/Algebra.htm

Edwards, E. (1990). *Algebra for Everyone.* Reston, VA: National Council of Teachers of Mathematics.

Long, L. (1998). *Painless Algebra.* Hauppauge, NY: Barron's Educational Series.

National Council of Teachers of Mathematics. (2000). *Principles and Standards for School Mathematics.* Reston, VA: National Council of Teachers of Mathematics.

National Council of Teachers of Mathematics (NCTM). (2004). *Standards and Expectations for Algebra.* Reston, VA: National Council of Teachers of Mathematics. Found online at: http://www.nctm.org

Freudenthal Institute at the University of Utrecht/ University of Wisconsin/NSF. *Math in Context.* http://showmecenter.missouri.edu/showme/mic.shtml Encyclopedia Britannica.

Web Resources

About Math
http://math.about.com/od/quadraticequation/

http://math.about.com/gi/dynamic/offsite.htm

Algebra Help
Algebra.help. (2001–2004) *Algebra Help.* Found online at: http://www.algebrahelp.com/index.jsp

Algebra Solutions
http://www.gomath.com/algebra.html

Awesome Library—Algebra
http://www.awesomelibrary.org/Classroom/Mathematics/Middle-High_School_Math/Algebra.html

Borenson, H. (2001–2004) *Hands on Equations.* Allentown, PA: Borenson and Associates. Found online at: http://www.borenson.com/?src=overture

Brennon, J. (2002) *Understanding Algebra.* Found online at: http://www.jamesbrennan.org/algebra/

Classzone Algebra 1
http://www.classzone.com/books/algebra_1/index.cfm

College Algebra Home Page West Texas A & M University
http://www.wtamu.edu/academic/anns/mps/math/mathlab/col_algebra/index.htm

http://www.wtamu.edu/academic/anns/mps/math/mathlab/col_algebra/col_alg_tut15_rateq.htm

Cool Math Sites
http://www.cte.jhu.edu/techacademy/web/2000/heal/mathsites.htm

Ed Helper.com
http://www.edhelper.com/algebra.htm

History of Algebra
http://www.ucs.louisiana.edu/~sxw8045/history.htm

References (cont.)

Holt, Rinehart and Winston Mathematics in Context
http://www.hrw.com/math/mathincontext/index.htm

Interactive Mathematic Miscellany and Puzzles
http://www.cut-the-knot.org/algebra.shtml

Introduction to Algebra
http://www.mathleague.com/help/algebra/algebra.htm

Math Archives: Topics in Mathematics, Algebra
http://archives.math.utk.edu/topics/algebra.html

Moses, B. *The Algebra Project.* Cambridge, MA: The Algebra Project, Inc.
http://www.algebra.org/index.html

Oracle Education Foundation Think Quest Library (2004) *Algebra.* Found online at: http://library.thinkquest.org/10030/algecon.htm

Purple Math
http://www.purplemath.com/modules/solvrtnl.htm

Reichman, H. and Kohn, M.(2004) *Math Made Easy.* Found online at: http://mathmadeeasy.com/algebra.html

Reliable Problem Solving in All Subjects That Use Mathematics for Problem Solving. Algebra, Physics, Chemistry … From Grade School to Grad School and Beyond
http://www2.hawaii.edu/suremath/intro_algebra.html

Show Me Center
http://www.showmecenter.missouri.edu/showme/

SOS Mathematics
http://www.sosmath.com/

http://www.sosmath.com/algebra/quadraticeq/complsquare/complsquare.html

Surfing the Net With Kids
http://www.surfnetkids.com/algebra.htm

The Math Forum Drexel University (1994–2004) *K–12 Internet Algebra Resources.* Philadelphia, PA: Found Online at: http://mathforum.org/algebra/k12.algebra.html

University of Akron Theoretical and Applied Mathematics
http://www.math.uakron.edu/~dpstory/mpt_home.html

Real Life Applications of Math

Applied Academics: Applications of Mathematics— Careers
http://www.bced.gov.bc.ca/careers/aa/lessons/math.htm

Exactly How is Math Used in Technology?
http://www.math.bcit.ca/examples/index.shtml

Mathematics Association of America—Careers
http://www.maa.org/careers/index.html

NASA Space Link
http://spacelink.msfc.nasa.gov/index.html